WOOD SMOKE AND PIGEON PIE

Joan Kent

CHIVERS LARGE PRINT
BATH

British Library Cataloguing in Publication Data available

This Large Print edition published by Chivers Press, Bath, 1996.

Published by arrangement with Century, Random House (UK) Limited.

U.K. Hardcover ISBN 0 7451 4776 3
U.K. Softcover   ISBN 0 7451 4777 1

Photoset, printed and bound in Great Britain by
Redwood Books, Trowbridge, Wiltshire

CONTENTS

'To inspire selfless love is to
become immortal.'

To MUM and DAD

INTRODUCTION

Dad said that all the money in the world could not purchase five seconds of sunshine during a wet harvest. It made hard cash sound like an insalubrious, unmentionable contagion from which we were utterly immune. He was right in his assertion that most of the wealthy people we knew were prone to moodiness, melancholia, or stomach ulcers. By my reckoning we had to be the happiest, healthiest folks for miles around.

We were a trifle light on affluence, even by the low financial standards of the late nineteen thirties. Mum, Dad and I had been sitting round the kitchen fire assessing our combined resources. With a hundred-acre farm to run between us, we established the fact that we were solvent to the extent of thirty-two shillings and sixpence.

My parents, both in their mid-sixties, never doubted our ability to weather 'Acts of God', crop failures, or any other agricultural disasters. I was seventeen then, working with my father, wanting no other way of life. Cottage-loaf shaped and five foot nothing, Mum had always seemed the epitome of perpetual motion in a floral pinny.

As the child of her middle age, Mum's 'late-hatched chick' growing up in the old farmhouse long after the rest of her brood of nine had left it, I could sense an increasing vulnerability about her. She needed shielding from her own belief that she could still work like two men. In some premonitory manner, our very close mother-and-daughter relationship had gradually changed. The protective aspect had become reserved.

To our financial credit, the stacked grain harvest was safely thatched and waiting for the threshing machine to arrive in our district. A substantial acreage of winter wheat was safely sown. Many of the flock of marauding wood pigeons that came to raid it ended up under the crust of a pigeon pie. When it came to feeding our stock and ourselves we were almost self sufficient. Our largest unavoidable expense was the load of coal with which to fuel the steam engine powering the threshing tackle. It seemed exorbitant at £2 a ton.

Where we were concerned, coal was a 'town' commodity bordering on the luxurious. The basic necessity for heating, cooking, or obtaining hot water to fill the zinc bath tub was simple—'First cut down your tree'.

Money from selling eggs, butter, or snared rabbits went to buy essentials. It seems strange to recall that the two items heading that list were bird-scaring cartridges and paraffin. Had Mum and Dad been asked to name their most invaluable possessions on that day when we had less than £2 to our credit, Mum would unhesitatingly have chosen the oil lamp with the globe that gleamed like sunshine through a stained glass window and transformed our kitchen table into the hub of our winter evening world.

Undoubtedly Dad would have chosen his sharp-toothed six-foot crosscut saw. We cut logs from dying or fallen fruit trees in the old orchard and kept the wood pile high. With the sweet scent of blazing cherry and apple wood filling the lamp-lit kitchen, we sat round the fire, warming our feet on the brass-topped fender, watching the wood smoke rising. Recalling other occasions when funds had been restricted, Dad related one anecdote, then another. Despite all the hard work and financial setbacks, we had discovered the basic necessities of happiness and were utterly content.

That other country world with its different values and dimensions disappeared so rapidly, yet it takes so little for a flood of memories to come streaming back.

A lone primrose by a roadside hedgerow; a flock of wood pigeon flying; the smell of wood smoke on the wind.

JOAN KENT
'Beam Ends'

SWEET SUNDAY

Lie-abed Sundays were a luxury unknown to us, as children. Inner cleanliness was a fetish with our Mum and her massive Saturday evening doses of liquorice and senna eliminated all hope of staying blanket-bound for very long after the dawn chorus had begun. Any ideas that a hurriedly-donned coat could retain the bed-warmed cosiness of the winceyette nightdress beneath it evaporated during the shivery scamper to the 'outback' at the bottom of the garden path. Breezes from all four quarters of heaven seemed to converge round that small draughty weather-boarded building. We learned young the wisdom of rising early and getting dressed fast.

In consequence, Sunday breakfast was

1

earlier than on weekdays. Yet while on weekdays time seemed to plod leadenfooted round the face of the clock in the village schoolroom, on Sundays the minutes and hours joined hands and ran.

My arrival in this world being an April Fool joke that Nature had played on an overworked, middle-aged, and utterly astonished woman, there was a seven-year gap between the youngest of my eight brothers and sisters and myself.

Those still living at home were all allocated their Sunday morning tasks. While the older ones fed livestock, or helped Mum in the farmhouse kitchen, my job was to gather wild watercress from the stream beyond Gipsy Corner.

Restricted only by the relative depth of water, and my gumboots, I could explore the rushy banks or wade beneath the low-branched willows where wild waterfowl hid, to collect the best cress that grew in the centre of the stream. Where the stream wandered on through open pasture, an inquisitive herd of dairy shorthorns often ambled over to glare their disapproval of the intruder splashing through their water supply. The semi-stagnant pools made by their hooves teemed with tadpoles in early springtime. My instant aquarium was a two-pound jam jar on a string.

I plodded around in the cold water collecting dainty little water snails, blissfully unaware that these were host to the larvae of a worm of infinitesimal size with revolting habits, and a keenness to establish residence inside anyone unfortunate enough to munch it with their watercress. Mum's drastic weekly cleansing doses must have destroyed any parasitic wrigglers, for no one in our family was ever stricken with the 'horrids'. We were told that, like horses that are fed on a plentiful supply of greenstuff, watercress would bring a smooth lustrous sheen to our hides when we ate it for Sunday tea.

If I had timed things nicely, I was back home in time to watch my Father's Sunday morning shave. It fascinated me to watch his leather-stropped, cut-throat razor scything through the soap-sud beard that made him look like a genial Father Christmas. I knew every laughter line etching the beloved weather-worn geography of his excessive face. Six-foot tall and broad shouldered, Dad seemed to be an invincible giant, incapable of injustice, underhandedness, or humbug. In all the subsequent years when we worked day-by-day, side-by-side, through times of tears and laughter, never once did my opinion of him change.

He had a dry sense of humour. A smile always lurked in his dark brown eyes. With his moustache trimmed, and all trace of bristles vanished, he would solemnly hand me his earthenware shaving mug with the solemn injunction: 'Be careful how you carry this, Jo. If you spill "whisker seeds" along the path instead of down in the gully, we'll grow coconut mats out there instead of grass'.

To me this seemed downright wasteful. If we could strain off the soapy water, we could make a fortune if we sold packets of 'whisker seeds' to bald headed men.

With his pipe in his mouth, a twelve-bore shotgun under his arm, and dressed in his Sunday corduroys, striped shirt and moleskin 'weskit', Dad was now ready for his weekly perambulation around the farm. This was his gate-leaning, slow-strolling time for contemplating everything that grew within our little hundred-acre world. A time to plan the following week's work, to feel if the soil was warming up for planting. A time, perhaps, to stop and try to convince a puzzled ewe that the strange orphan in the pen beside her, which had been draped in her dead lamb's skin, was really her own offspring.

The silence of deserted fields was scarcely disturbed by mother and baby talk from the lambing pasture, distant laying hens triumphantly cackling, or the sound of Sunday morning church bells. If all farm labour stopped on Sundays, the rooks and pigeons did not. Marauding wood pigeons were our particular problem, raiding the corn fields, gorging on our cattle kale. They would rise up and fly over to the nearby woods to re-muster to the attack when they thought it was safe. Dad sometimes waited for them, hiding in a natural hollow beneath a low-branched beech tree on the bank between the woodlands and our fields.

The camouflage of the beech tree hide must have been almost perfect, for one Sunday we were treated to the spectacle of our parson's sister—over-sized and well over fifty, furtively hurrying along the edge of the wood. The 'sick headaches' to which she was prone often made her too unsteady to attend her brother's church services. Watching her dispose of a carrier-bag full of empty gin bottles down the rabbit holes that honeycombed the bank, we realised for the first time the cause of her indisposition.

Silence and utter immobility were essential when the sound of planing pigeon wings warned that they were swooping in to the attack. After an ear-splitting report, Dad would stand rubbing his right shoulder, for our old shot gun had a recoil like the kick of a maladjusted mule.

Despite his marksmanship, we never seemed to reduce the pigeon population. We had more than our fair share of pigeon pies. There is a country belief that pigeon meat has a dramatically binding effect on the human constitution. We had no need to worry. Remembering why we had to rise early every Sunday, we knew that our Mum had found the perfect antidote to that.

5

There was always an extra plate filled with Sunday dinner. This Mum kept warm over a pan of water on the kitchen stove. We used to tease her about the old chap who called to eat it. But she, having known bad times, believed that we were never too hard up to spare food for those less fortunate.

We called him 'Cockle Billy', an old man eking out some sort of living by selling shellfish which he collected along the sea shore.

He had a Sunday round, walking miles to sell cooked winkles that he carried in a gipsy basket covered with a none-too-clean white cloth.

I respected Cockle Billy, for he once charmed away my warts. He would eat his dinner just inside the back door. And when he left there was always a quart of winkles in Mum's yellow mixing bowl on the scullery shelf.

While Cockle Billy munched his way through what was probably the only decent meal he had had all week, I was reluctantly getting dressed up in my Sunday best to attend the afternoon Bible Class. There 'Parson's Sister' tried hard to drive me along the paths of righteousness but, try as I might, I always seemed to lose track along the way. The genealogical sequence of the Old Testament never inspired my soul; I could never remember, much less recite, who begat whom.

'Parson's Sister' would rave and shout, her

breath smelling of peppermint and drink. One Sunday afternoon she was particularly abusive, calling me 'idiot girl' and asking where my brains were. I told her they were in the rabbit warren alongside some empty gin bottles. Her response was to apply her heavy Bible with some force to the top of my head, instead of instructing me in its contents in the usual way.

Her God lived within hidebound covers. Mine sang in his heaven and rippled with laughter, like a breeze passing over a field of ripening wheat. After the Bible Class incident I was left to find my way to salvation by whatever path I chose.

Released from the old schoolroom, I was free to amble home slowly, knowing that when I got there I would be greeted by overpoweringly affectionate visiting aunts in their best costumes and Sunday hats. This then was the pattern of the sweet Sundays of my childhood, with watercress, winkles, and a wedge of Mum's cut-and-come-again cake for tea.

OLD INDESTRUCTIBLE

Mum said she would have to be sitting on an iceberg in her petticoat before she would pay the exorbitant price of 5/11¾d for a flimsy shop-bought jumper having less wool to it than one would find on a skinned sheep's leg.

It would be cheaper to make one. And it would give her something to occupy her time when the winter evening lamps were lit.

Because knitting was a pastime that she did not usually indulge in, she chose a plain uncomplicated style.

Doggedly persevering with the plaining and purling, she knitted on, although the complexity of the design completely baffled her. Then she realised that, like a tree in autumn, her knitting pattern book had shed some of its leaves.

By that stage part of the pattern of a 'Cosy Camisole For The Fuller Figure' had been incorporated into its construction. By this time nearly all the 'unrepeatable bargain offer' of scarlet wool, bought specially to make the jumper, had been used up.

Such trifles would never daunt my mother. She had spent too long knitting it to start unpicking, nor would she admit defeat. A few ounces of faith, and some wool in a contrasting colour, were all that was needed to transform it into something wearable.

Her task completed, Mum held it up for family approval. None of her five daughters knew who would be the recipient. Without exception, we sat there dumbly praying. 'Let it not be me!'

It was an impressive garment.

Mistaking silence for awestruck admiration, Mum smiled happily, then passed her handiwork over to my sister Nora, a gifted girl with scholastic and artistic talents. Mum believed that such gifts must predispose her to 'having a weak chest'.

Thankful that I was the youngest, too scrawny and too small to have really been in the running, I encouraged Nora to try the garment on.

Mum's ingenuity had excelled itself. In contrast to the main part, knitted in scarlet, she had used an aggressively discordant yellow to

9

finish off the gathered top of one baggy puff-sleeve.

A kind of pie-frill that held the neckline together was in the same stark colour, and in an inspirational moment she had added a deep band of yellow, lacy crochet around the bottom edge—to lengthen it and to 'add the finishing touch'.

Despite Mum's assertion that to buy an original-designed model in a shop would cost a small fortune, Nora wore it somewhat reluctantly for a couple of Sundays. Then it was washed.

From the moment it sank under the suds in the wooden washtub, Mum knew that disaster was overtaking her work of art.

She squeezed it, wrung it, and hung it out to dry on the plum trees. She pressed, stretched and pulled it sideways, but to no avail.

Scrutinizing the long thin tubular garment, Mum made a decision and Nora's trend-setting Sunday jumper became my everyday winter dress.

As some sort of consolation, Nora volunteered to do a length of French knitting to thread through the pattern holes around the middle, thus forming a sort of belt to take in the slack. This was made in navy sock wool, but by then I didn't care.

Mum was reluctant to remove the crochet edging around the hemline because it would help to keep my legs warm, but it made anything but the smallest steps impossible and was liable to trip me up if I tried to run.

I loathed that dress, praying each time it was washed that it would perish. But as I grew, it grew with me, and when there seemed to be some hope that I had at last outpaced it, back went the yellow band of crochet lace around the hem. It seemed indestructible.

Age, and the washtub, added strength to its fibres, giving it the same hard-wearing qualities as asbestos. The texture felt about as soft to my bare skin.

Complaining about it only provoked Mum into the oft-repeated theme that plenty of shivering girls would be glad to wear so warm a garment. I nurtured the secret hope that one so desperately deprived would come my way, for heaven knew that I would gladly give it up at once.

The opportunity came on a spring morning, made glorious because both winter and 'Old Indestructible' were cast aside for the next three seasons and because the weather was ideal for planting corn. The whole routine of the household revolved around the fact that the men were sowing oats and barley.

The rooks that lived in the tall elms circled over Barn Field watching the work in progress. Every now and then they flew back to give their nesting mates raucous and detailed reports on the foolish humans who were scattering enough food to feed the rookery for weeks.

11

Mum and I were detailed to make a realistic-looking scarecrow to frighten the marauding birds away. A pair of old overalls stuffed with straw and a pitchfork-handle spine gave the basic human shape. By the time it was dressed in Dad's old blue sweater and topped by a painted sock for a face, it only needed the cap that a fleeing poacher had abandoned in Ten Acres and a pair of leaky 'wellies' to make it very lifelike indeed.

We were preparing to load it on a barrow to wheel it to the cornfield in triumph, when we saw the old scissors grinder pushing his portable grindstone down the farm track.

Some yards behind him walked a round-shouldered woman. Mum found several old steel knives that needed sharpening and also the scissors that served to cut anything from chicken wire to Dad's hair.

The woman stood pouring water from a beer bottle over the grindstone as her man worked a foot-treadle.

'Terrible weather we've had, ain't it, Lady?' she said. 'The little'un's been racked with the cold and wet.'

Mum looked puzzled until I nodded towards a thinly-clad, runny-nosed little girl with a mop of unkempt hair, following behind.

'You don't have any warm clothes as would fit her, do you lady? Something too small for your bonny girl?'

To my knowledge, no one before had ever

called me bonny, but I couldn't warm to the woman's wheedling tone.

Mum would never send beggars away empty-handed, and if anyone told her she was a sitting target for scroungers she replied in a small quiet voice that would break your heart to hear it, that she herself had once known real hunger and want.

I was sent upstairs to search in the old wooden chest on the landing to find something outgrown, but warm.

This provided the chance to get rid of a hoard of despised liberty bodices and scratchy woollen vests. I found a purple jumper of my sister's that was lying around waiting for me to grow and bequeathed it to the scissor grinder's wife. All it needed now was to find something warm and woolly for her daughter.

Hiding its hideousness beneath the other cast-off clothing, I put my knitted winter dress into the newspaper-wrapped bundle. Then I watched the trio's departure, content that I had got rid of Old Indestructible at last.

We planted the scarecrow in the oat field, then Mum and I went to the edge of the wood to begin our annual ritual of picking bunches of primroses and packing them in moss.

These Mum posted to a city hospital as a gesture of thanksgiving. Once, in her far-off days of want she had stayed within its walls where, for one nightmare spring, she had seen no flowers at all.

As we were returning, the scissor grinder and his family passed us, the little girl enveloped in a dark-blue, too-large garment made of wool. We realised where it had come from when we walked across the cornfield.

Dad's sweater had been removed from the scarecrow and so had the poacher's cap. Beside the scarecrow lay a torn newspaper parcel, containing a woolly vest and my hideous old winter dress.

For an awful moment I thought that Mum would take it home and wash it ready for next winter, but she decided that the scissor grinder's child was probably infested with nits. Instead, she put it on the scarecrow, and used the vest as a turban for its sock head.

Old Indestructible served as an effective bird scarer for two planting seasons and ended up in the hedge, providing plentiful building material for nesting birds and a maternity home for mice.

THE GLORY HOLE

Mum called it 'getting an early start', which meant that while roosters in the back yard were still crowing we were on our way to the common, walking through still, chill, dew that hung in shimmering crystals on the bracken, soaking the hems of our dresses and our shoes.

We were on one of our annual blackberry picking expeditions, carrying as many picking baskets as my mother could muster. Each of us carried a hooked stick to pull down any ripe fruit that would otherwise be out of reach.

As we reached the bank of laden bushes, we were reminded that 'Folk too lazy to gather what the good Lord had sent to feed them, deserved to be hungry'.

Playing, instead of picking, would mean less

15

jam or bramble jelly on our bread at teatimes, fewer winter blackberry puddings or pies from the fruit that Mum would bottle, and definitely no sugar-soaked berries from the bottom of the wine crock when the cleared ruby liquid was fit to strain into narrow-necked earthenware jars.

'Winey-berries', served by Mum with vanilla junket, seemed to me the ultimate in high-living. They would have been the mainstay of my diet had I been a rich heiress and not the youngest of a large and hard-up farming family.

On this occasion, we had finished our bottle of home-made lemonade and eaten our pasties long before mid-day. We had also grown peevish, parched and sick of picking. There was fruit in plenty left on the bushes, but by then we had filled more baskets than we had arms to carry them home.

Using a hedge stake strong enough to support the weight of the more cumbersome of the baskets, my brothers carried the bulk of our harvest supported between them, while the rest of us struggled along with what we could.

According to the corn-store scale, we had picked almost 200lbs of fruit between us and, after a hurried Bubble-and-Squeak dinner, those not fully occupied with extracting thorns from sore fingers were washing and polishing glass jam jars and 7lb earthenware pots.

Mum, resting before she started jam-making in earnest, was pouring herself a cup of tea

16

from the old, hob-blackened pot, when the travelling oilman drove into the yard. Lamps being our only means of lighting, the standing order for paraffin and candles made him one of the few regular callers at the farm. So courtesy demanded that he be invited in and offered a cup of tea.

He sat in the kitchen, smelling of turpentine, soap, floor polish and paraffin, and saw the baskets of fruit that we had picked. 'My word!' he exclaimed, 'Seeing that the jam factory in Castle Lane is offering 3d a pound for blackberries, fresh picked, I reckon that lot would come to a fair week's wage.'

Mum thought at first that he was joking. But realising that he was in earnest she did some frantic mental arithmetic and announced a change of plan.

We were to collect basins, bags or anything we could fill with berries and return to the common, picking where the fruit was thickest until teatime, while she hitched a lift to the jam factory with as many baskets as the oilman's van had room to take.

In an instant she was scraping stray wisps of hair under her hat and impaling the purple roses on it with enormous hat-pins. Before we had time to argue she was sitting on the Sunlight soap box, with strings of brushes, tin kettles, and pot-menders swaying around her, as the van went down the lane.

The market day bus brought her back soon

17

after teatime and she walked up from Lockley Bottom with several empty baskets and a huge parcel, liberally tied with thick white string.

The fruit she had taken into town had put more than the average farmhand's weekly wage into Mum's pocket, and when Dad came in she proudly told him that the mysterious parcel was a special 'Bargain Buy' from the paint and hardware store in the High Street. The contents would enable her to tackle an improvement she had dreamed about for years.

It was a job lot of wallpaper, 12 rolls for 3s, left over, so the assistant hinted, from decorating Her Ladyship's private sitting-room at The Hall.

Avoiding the basins, baskets and boxes of blackberries that were waiting to be dealt with in the kitchen, she carefully extracted one roll from the parcel, daring us to come near it with our fruit-stained hands. Dad, looking at the eye-swivelling mixture of orange, green, blue and purple, said that a bit of blackberry juice might calm it down, or, at least, would never show.

Violent rain overnight washed out all hope of harvesting or blackberry gathering the next morning, but Mum, removing the rows of jars filled with jam and jelly from the kitchen table, announced that she intended to put some of the newly-acquired paper on the walls.

'Which walls?' Dad asked, struck by the

18

awful thought that Mum had visions of papering the kitchen. Mum said that she was sick of seeing the patchy, flaking, yellow ochre walls in the passage.

The fact that the passage extended from the kitchen door, along the back of the house, past the scullery and dairy to end at the doorway to the narrow back stairs, meant little to Mum.

The kitchen table became a pasting board where lengths of the new paper were spread with home-made flour-and-water paste laced with size. It smelled awful, and the paper seemed more aggressively garish in daylight.

Worse than that, the pattern was so enormous that each length cut meant lopping off a yard, if it was to match its neighbour, and this Mum regarded as wicked waste.

Consequently, the vines that twined across one width of the paper were lopped off short at the join. Birds of Paradise that should have perched on the branches, appeared to have head transplants on to pomegranate bodies. Strolling peacocks seemed to be pecking at depleted bunches of grapes.

Dad, peering in at the door in passing, dared to comment that a sight of that paper was enough to put both man and beast clean off their food. Mum haughtily reminded him that what was fit to grace the aristocratic walls up at The Hall was fit for the kitchen passage, and it certainly brightened the old place up.

But Mum was having problems. The walls

were so uneven that the strips of paper were hanging diagonally instead of vertically and in some places refusing to stick to the wall at all. Watched by offspring trailing streamers from the trimmed edges, she thumped and smoothed away with a soft-bristled brush. In tackling one particularly obstinate section, she pushed the brush through the paper, plaster, wall and all.

The brush fell with a thud somewhere in the void beyond the wall, and one of us was detailed to go running for my father.

Realising that any space behind the wall must lie between the passage and the wide old kitchen chimney, Dad enlarged the hole enough to put his head and arm through. By the light of a candle he saw a narrow but long alcove, with the stonework of the chimney narrowing inward and upward to make extremely long and effective shelves.

Mum, seeing the stonework, immediately decided that she had found the ideal place for fermenting wines, even damp-free enough to store her jam. Nothing would suffice but that the alcove be re-opened. The plywood door that Dad made to fasten over the entrance got a covering coat of Mum's 'jungle' paper, too.

We called it The Glory Hole, and apart from the wine crocks and jam jars that lined its shelves, anything and everything that might one day 'come in useful' was stored within its depths. Long after the 'jungle' paper peeled off the other walls it still stuck, limpet-fast, to The

Glory Hole's plywood door.

When my old home changed owners again recently, one of the attractions that boosted it in value was its 'possible historical connections'. I hardly like to tell the new occupant that the stains on the stonework in the alcove he believes to be a priest's hiding place, have no sinister connections.

They were made when the yeast in Mum's blackberry wine fermented over, in the days when we preserved the fruits of summer and The Glory Hole shelves were stacked with homemade wine and delicious jam.

MILLER'S LANE

If being the after-thought of a large family meant the drawback of hand-me-down clothes, it had its compensations too.

As soon as I was old enough to be trusted to keep my shoe laces tied, my nose wiped, and my drawers dry, my over-worked Mum was quite willing to let Dad or one of my three brothers take me with them as they worked around the farm.

With eight of her nine offspring in their 'teens and twenties, Mum had far too much to do to cluck around me like an old hen with a late-hatched chick.

Her common sense gave me a priceless gift of having the freedom to explore unhindered, a guileless, magical world where I could dig around beside a hawthorn hedge, convinced that the summer rainbow shimmering above it signified that a pot of gold lay buried underneath.

A toad, disturbed in his slumber by my digging, just had to be an enchanted prince, placed under a spell by the witch that I had long suspected of dwelling in the hollow ash tree by the pond.

My brothers said that a family of woodpeckers were responsible for the strange tapping noises down inside the trunk. But I distrusted the scary way its branches waved and beckoned like a scarecrow's arms, and the scowling face shaped by the knotholes in its bark.

In constant expectation of a transformation scene I fed my toad-prince slugs and hid him in a 7lb stone jam jar until he spat in my face and escaped.

If I grew tired of plodding around, my brothers would perch me on whatever horse-drawn implement they were using. Queen-like, I rode on hay wagons, timber tugs, corn drills, and dung carts.

If it rained, a corn sack turned in corner-to-corner made a windproof, waterproof, thick-cowled cape, large enough to keep a small girl snug and dry. In this I could be Red Riding Hood, a monk, a goblin, or anything else I chose.

Sitting on my brother Harold's coat on the

23

floor of the tip-cart watching the dust-brown ribbon of Miller's Lane unwind beneath the tailboard, mine was a hedge-high view of wonderland, not just a ride in a farm cart along a commonplace country road.

Miller's Lane ran straight and narrow to begin with, its verges churned into a muddy slough by the hooves of the dairy herd that commuted between their pasture and the milking sheds twice a day. To meet them in the narrows was somewhat overwhelming, while oncoming carts met each other like jousting knights.

Wheel nave to wheel nave, there was just enough room to pass, but it took courage when one wheel-rim, forced off the trackway, meant a floundering horse and a nearside axle deep in mud.

Once we had run the gauntlet of the narrows, the lane widened and changed direction, the roadside ditch joining forces with a fussy little rushing stream. This kept the road company down a hill, but beside a cottage that could only be approached by a narrow foot-bridge, it altered course and hurried back across the fields.

The stream had no name that I knew of, and since the dear old couple in the cottage were named Jordan, the Jordan river it became.

In Sunday school I learned of St John the Baptist's activities in the River Jordan, and realised that the river was on our very doorstep, as it were. A few Sunday school cronies joined me in a grand baptismal scheme.

It was tadpole time, with the summer an eternity away. Shivering, clad only in our cotton knickers, we ceremoniously dunked ourselves in the brook in Miller's Lane, watching our sins and Emmy's Sunday hat float down the stream.

Pure in mind and spirit, we hurried home carrying our wet pants, but two irate mothers complained to Mum. Joan the Baptist's ministry came to a painful, sudden end.

At the bottom of the hill the surface of Miller's Pond was a carpet of green slime, the home of monster-sized newts. Sometimes we would take the carts into the pond to let the water saturate and swell the shrunken 'felloes'—the outer circles of the wooden wheels.

We kept to the edge though, knowing that the viscous mud in the middle had become the watery grave of our old 'Tin Lizzie' lorry when it ran away from my brother's driving on Miller's Hill.

At the top of the hill was a sight I would still cross counties to see. Unless there was a dead calm, with no wind to puff them into motion, the 50ft-long, white-painted sails of Mr Barker's mill scythed through the air like a myriad of startled starling's wings. From the road one could hear the pulsating sound of the mill-wheel grinding corn.

In a stiff breeze the whole structure vibrated, the timbers of the framework creaked, the grinding machinery overhead kept an hypnotic rhythm with the whirling sails.

If we called at the mill for flour or cattle food, I would stand on the loading floor completely over-awed.

'She'm talking to us all the time, girl,' old Tom Barker would say, and just as sailors on full-rigged windjammers were aware that they were governed by sea and sky, so does the sensation of being in a working windmill make one feel part of earth and air.

From Tom Barker I learned the difference between 'stoneground', 'middlings', 'sharps', and 'bran', and that the expression 'setting the Thames on fire' had nothing to do with the river, but was derived from a miller's wooden-framed sieve called a temse, which became extremely hot if the mill was running fast.

One gale-lashed winter day, Mr Barker sent an urgent message to all the neighbouring farmers to send him any grinding corn they had. He had to keep the mill running to prevent the force of the wind from tearing out the cogs or twisting the main shaft. To try to brake it, or let it run on without corn in the head bins, meant that the mill could easily catch fire.

'She'm getting cussed and middlin' headstrong in her old age,' Tom Barker complained. It could not have been very long after that when the old mill actually blew down.

Nevertheless, we had a constant reminder of its existence. With all her bread-making and cooking, Mum bought flour in 140lb cotton sacks. Empty, these began a new life as tea-towels, and each bore a faithful replica of the old mill, with T. Barker, Esquire, Miller, printed on them in black.

A mile or so beyond the mill a single track railway line crossed Miller's Lane. The crossing keeper lived in a converted railway carriage beside the track. This I believed to be a socially superior residence because it bore the gold-painted words 'First Class' along its side.

The keeper was a keen gardener. Local children would collect flower seeds for him to plant. From snowdrop time to the last frost-browned chrysanthemum, the banks of the cutting and the track side were a carpet of bloom.

Just beyond the level-crossing we would turn in at the field gate of Long End. This was a narrow tract of land Dad hired because its sheltered position grew the first early bite of clover or lucerne. My brothers scythed this crop to take back home to feed as 'greenmeat' to the stock.

On the south-facing bank, primroses and white violets grew, wild strawberries ripened, and squat little lizards basked in the summer sun.

Here my eldest brother, pausing from

27

sharpening his scythe, would recapture for my benefit his own childhood adventure of Long End.

It was just grass pasture then, and Harold, rising ten in the last year of the Kaiser's war, was sent to Long End before he went to school to check that all was well with a cow and a new calf.

It was a misty morning, and when Harold got there he saw a uniformed man unsuccessfully trying to milk the cow. At the far end of the meadow, shrouded by mist, someone was hammering on wood.

The uniformed man offered Harold a bar of chocolate if he would fill a hip flask with milk. While Harold obliged, the man, who was then joined by a companion, asked about the direction of the main railway line and the nearest towns. Fearful of being late for school, he took the chocolate and ran. As he closed the gate he saw in the thinning mist the vague outline of a two-winged plane.

When Harold tried to explain to his teacher what had happened, she imagined that he had come up with a new excuse for being late—until she noticed that the wrapper of the chocolate she had confiscated was printed in German.

By the time the village policeman and his reinforcements had reached Long End on their bikes, the aviators were gone. The chocolate was 'evidence' that Harold never saw again.

Today, both railway line and level-crossing are gone and it takes about four minutes to travel along the lane by car. It is narrow, with no passing places, and nowhere that one can linger.

I'm glad that I once was given time to stare and wonder, discovering the magic of places like Miller's Lane.

THE DIVIDING LINE

On that last day of Emmy Price's childhood we sat in the drowsy atmosphere of coke fumes and tight-closed windows, hands on our nodding heads, watching the sluggard hands of the schoolroom clock.

Twenty minutes, or thirty if the irascible schoolmaster was in a particularly bad humour, then we would bellow our gabbling way through 'Lord Dismiss Us' and enjoy the blessed relief of end-of-term.

Wrath-provoking coughing, sneezing, or fidgeting would delay our liberation, so we sat subservient, still as petrified field mice, trying to judge the mood of the schoolmaster by the aspect of his hawk-like face.

He looked up, with an expression to which

the downward drooping corners of his mouth were totally unaccustomed, and smilingly invited Emmy Price to stand up on her chair.

Suspicious that in these last moments of her schooldays she was to be the butt of his sarcastic wit, Emmy, blushing scarlet and trembling, obeyed his command.

The schoolmaster then informed us that we were looking at a singularly fortunate girl.

At an inspection visit by 'Her Ladyship' and a party of school governors a few days earlier, Emmy's ability to recite the books of the Bible in the correct sequence, forward and backward, had been well received.

The schoolmaster announced that 'Her Ladyship' was so impressed with this performance that she had personally selected Emmy to train for domestic service in the kitchens of The Hall.

According to the schoolmaster, this honour proved that rewards awaited diligent scholars. Emmy was such an example to her fellow pupils that we were permitted to applaud.

Tearful with adolescent embarrassment, Emmy stood shuffling her scuffed shoes on the chair seat, her startlingly fair hair held back by a shoe-lace ribbon, holes in her woollen stockings, and the black hem of her dress unstitched.

The Price family accounted for an eighth of the school register, Emmy having seven younger brothers and sisters attending school

31

with her. All had tow coloured hair, looking alike as pods of various sizes growing on a row of peas.

Released from school, Emmy still wept as she buttoned coats, tied broken boot-laces, wiped noses, and found missing dinner bags, then shepherded the younger Prices out of the school yard to begin their long trek home.

I failed to understand why she could cry over leaving school when the only words of encouragement she had ever received there had been within minutes of her departure.

Two years her junior, still believing that 'Lords and Ladies' led a life of perpetual gargantuan banquets, I foresaw Emmy's culinary future as being filled with a surfeit of gammon steaks, salmon, quail in aspic, fish and chips, ice cream and jelly, and, consequently, very bright indeed.

I was soon disillusioned. Emmy's aunt had worked in the dark rambling basement kitchens and sculleries of The Hall. She told Emmy tales of stone slab floors heaving with cockroaches, beetles, and mice at night, and of a chilly thick-walled stillroom that had a 'haunt'.

'I don't want to work in their miserable old kitchens. I want to be a nurse and deliver babies,' Emmy wept.

On a bonfire of unsaleable remnants from a jumble sale, Emmy had found a book on first aid and basic anatomy. Smoke-spoiled as it was, it became her most prized possession despite her parents' assertion that it was not 'proper reading matter' for a young girl.

She studied it avidly, believing that the fund of knowledge it contained would assist her efforts to obtain work in the nursing profession, even if she had to start by scrubbing hospital floors.

I couldn't visualise the prospect of school without gentle Emmy bathing scraped knees, defending the smaller ones from bullies, or cosseting bewildered new infants howling to go back home to Mum.

How her mother would manage when she went into service was beyond my imagination, for beside the eight Price children on the school register there were three smaller ones at home.

My observation on this point made Emmy more cheerful, encouraging her to impart the secret that her mother was not, as I'd been led to believe, indulging in an inflationary diet of radishes, haricot beans and new bread. Her increased size was due to the fact that baby number twelve was due around Whitsuntide.

No one even consulted Emmy's wishes on her future. She left school on Maundy Thursday and because there was a house party at The Hall over the holiday weekend, started work on the Saturday before Easter Day.

For weeks, news of Emmy was secondhand and scanty. Among the seven schoolgoing Prices, the ministrations of their maternal-

33

minded sister were sadly missed.

Then, early on Whit Sunday morning, I heard the chattering of a multitude of Prices coming along the lane. When they got to the farmyard I realised that Emmy was with them. She said she had been allowed home for the day.

'Tomorrow too, if the new baby is a long time coming.'

I asked how the unexpected holiday had come about.

'The district nurse phoned Madam, personal-like, last evening,' Emmy said. 'Then, after I had lit the kitchen ranges about five o'clock this morning, Dad was allowed to come over on his bike and fetch me home. Now I've been told to keep all the children out of the way until bedtime, so we're going on a picnic for the day. Coming?'

Nine walking Prices plus two pram-bound infants accompanied me to the farmhouse kitchen to ask Mum if she would let me go. She consented, and gave us bread, cheese, apples and cold rice pudding solid enough to cut into wedges for our picnic fare. This Emmy stowed amongst the nibbled rusks, blanket fluff, and spare baby pants stuffed in the well of the old-fashioned pram. She replaced the padded boards, the soggy mattress, settled the two soggier-seated infants, then we were off.

Asked where they wanted to be taken, the

34

family were unanimously in favour of the beach. The nearest coast, six miles distant, was nothing but marsh-grass, sea and sky.

We saw Cockle Billy collecting shellfish and walked along with him, following the outgoing tide. The memory of that Saturday still conjures up a picture of sunlight on a smooth sea, the sound of happy children and Emmy laughing with the rest.

At church on Whit Sunday morning the ladies of the congregation were agog with the obstetric details of the birth of Mrs Price's new-born son.

They all agreed that Her Ladyship had shown generous consideration in allowing Emmy to have two whole days off, without deducting any of her five shillings a week pay. Emmy, they said, was an extremely fortunate girl.

Thinking of my old school-mate, whose burning ambition was to go nursing and who was now pot-scrubber in the sunless basement sculleries of The Hall I wondered where good fortune came in.

The finality of a fourteenth birthday dividing line between the freedom of Emmy's childhood and having to go into service, seemed appalling.

I walked home from church with one of Emmy's little sisters. One braid of her unkempt hair had escaped from its ragged ribbon. She asked if I could replait it, the way

Emmy did.

She was runny-nosed and slightly smelly. I had no idea why I clung to her and cried.

MUM'S CHEEPING CHILDREN

The walled garden was a self-perpetuating wilderness of scent and colour. Old-fashioned flowers crowded in between bushes of purple lilac, flowering currant and syringa, blossoming where they could. Year after year the yellow gillyflowers struck tenuous roots within the crevices of the weather-worn walls and still managed to bloom.

No one tried to tame our flower garden. It was seldom dug or hoed; because each corner of it was easily seen from Mum's kitchen window, it became a nursery for her hens each spring.

Fussy fowls in make-shift coops between the bushes clucked at their adventurously-minded chicks exploring the jungle world beneath the

37

peony plants, well camouflaged from preying sparrow hawks or hungry crows.

Mum regarded each broody hen as a challenge. It somehow reaffirmed her belief in the bounty of nature that she could place a hen on thirteen eggs in an old nesting box, and three weeks later increase her poultry stock by a 'baker's dozen' of day-old chicks.

She always set thirteen eggs in the traditional pattern of 'one-three-five-three-one' because old wives believed that a sitting hen would turn them in that pattern safely every night.

To vary the number was asking for a nest of addled eggs, or the hen might cast the whole lot from the nest. Worse than that, she could lose interest half way through the incubation period and let the eggs go cold.

Any unusual disturbance, perhaps a predatory rat, could have the same effect. Many a time we missed out on dinner because Mum had been too busy coping with a chicken crisis to worry about food.

The fate of a hen that had 'stood-off' a clutch of eggs was sealed by the black celluloid ring wound round its leg. This meant that come winter, when money was short and butcher's meat dear, another boiling fowl would find its way into the iron stewpot on the kitchen stove. No chicken would be given a second chance to desert its helpless young, if Mum knew what was what.

The heavy brass fender around the kitchen

fire was her polished pride, and heaven help anyone who dared to sully its surface with a muddy boot, or placed a cold, stockinged foot on the warmth of its flat top rail.

But if Mum discovered a clutch of 'stood-off' eggs, the nearest we were allowed to approach the fire was a rag hearth-rug's width away. Taking pride of place and most of the room on the top rail of the brass fender was a gipsy-made willow basket, lined with an old flannel nightie that had hung, tucked away out of sight, on the string airing line beneath the mantel fringe in preparation for a life or death emergency such as this.

Mum would come solemn-faced into the kitchen, carefully carrying the abandoned eggs in her gathered-up pinafore, supporting and warming them with one arm and with the other sheltering them from chill breezes.

Kneeling like a suppliant at an altar, she gently placed them on the warm flannel in the basket. After about an hour, she would demand absolute silence for a few minutes, and the more crafty of her children knew that this was the time to give the kitchen a wide berth.

One by one, she would pick up the eggs, making clicking noises with her tongue, and holding it close to her ear. This, she swore, was an infallible method of knowing if the embryo chicks had survived.

'If you say the right things, a chick will answer,' she would say to her disbelieving children.

Sometimes the eggs would need a week or more before they were due to hatch. Throughout that time our home life hinged on keeping the fender warm, but not too hot, and eliminating chick-destroying draughts, under the supervision of an otherwise absent-minded Mum.

'Hatching Day' meant meals at unpredictable hours, while Mum concentrated on damping down the eggs with warm water and reassuring the occupants that they would soon be strong enough to peck their way to freedom through shell-thin imprisoning walls. Only when the whole clutch was accounted for could we hope for any semblance of normal routine.

It was not from entirely unselfish motives that Dad thought he might stretch finances far enough to invest in a small incubator. But Mum would have none of it.

Her hand-reared chicks brought Mum a crop of problems, convinced as they were that she was their mother-hen.

Having spent their first few days in an apple box on the hearth rug, they were transferred to a safe coop-and-run in the garden during the day, returning to their hay-box nursery at night.

Whenever Mum walked up the garden path she was greeted by a group of cheeping chicks. And now, whenever purple lilac blooms I often recall one washday in the old walled garden, with every bush blossoming scented flowers and cotton tea towels. Beneath a clothes line full of billowing sheets, my mother once stood with a crowd of yellow chicks hopping in and out of the laundry basket and perching on her feet.

Sometimes a freelance hen went off to some secluded spot and hatched out a brood of chicks alone. The Prodigal Son was accorded much the same sort of welcome from his father, as such a chicken received from Mum.

The old rooster did his best to show the Rhode Island Reds of his harem just who ruled the roost, but it was obvious that the brilliant plumage of the younger chickens evolved through over-amorous pheasants becoming too familiar with his more flighty wives. Mum's hens were not brilliant egg producers, but, by Heaven, she raised some fine-feathered birds.

It was probably the pheasant strain that sometimes made more hens off-lay and broody than Mum could manage to set on eggs, but country people are resourceful. The problem was solved as soon as it arose.

The answer was 'His Lordship's' gamekeeper, a man whose 'broody hen scheme' was a piece of rural financial wizardry, because everyone believed that they had gained something from it, while he still managed to make a profit for himself.

It worked like this.

Since pheasants hatching in the wild are vulnerable to predators, their eggs were collected up and placed under broody hens for hatching.

For each hen acquired for this purpose 'His Lordship' allowed the gamekeeper a grant of one pound. In turn the gamekeeper bought the 'cluck' hen for fifteen shillings. When at the end of the breeding season, the pheasants were safely reared he sold the hen back to its former owner for five shillings. He was happy, having made a profit of ten shillings on the deal. 'His Lordship' was happy, for he had four or five extra brace of pheasants to shoot at—and generally miss.

Mum too was happy, having gained ten shillings, plus her hen, returned fat on 'His Lordship's' corn, and on the point of lay.

There can be few other monetary deals where no-one loses out, and if I met a financial wizard with the ability of that gamekeeper today, I would nominate him to help run the country when the next general election comes along.

THE POND IN THE WOOD

Shielded by the tall reeds that threatened to engulf it, Ladies Pool lay sombre, secretive and shady in the valley of the woods.

Brambles, head-high bracken and rosebay willowherb conspired to block the steep path descending between the birch woods on the hillside. Stout footwear and a determined disregard for mud and midges were needed to follow the oozing, squelchy path beside the stream.

Generations of village elders have warned young people that this smoke-haunted, lonely place is best avoided. Generations of disobedient children have been drawn towards it by stories of the monster in its murky depths.

Years would elapse with no sign of its

activities, but groups of inquisitive youngsters would embark on expeditions, hoping either to catch, or to catch sight of, the giant fish or eel in Ladies Pool.

One day Bill Budd, the thatcher, cutting reeds along the pond edge, reported that he had watched a dabchick disappear with scarce a ripple of the pondweed, and within minutes a swimming vole met the same unexpected fate.

Later, sitting quietly eating his elevenses, Bill saw the predator basking in the shallows within inches of his feet.

'It was a girt old fish, long as my arm but a durned sight thicker, with a sharp row of teeth and eyes as mean as a hungry wolf,' Bill told an audience of youngsters, which included my brother Stan.

Stan said he had half-a-mind to go there and try to catch it but it didn't sound the sort of fish you could tackle with a length of button-thread and a bent pin.

Not being of the stuff that solitary explorers were made of, Stan hoped that other boys would clamour to go along with him. They did not, but Billy Wells said he knew where Slippy, the poacher, had set some fish hooks baited with raisins to catch game from His Lordship's coverts.

Billy came running back, triumphantly carrying six fish hooks and a length of fishing line that Slippy had carelessly dropped.

Faced with the prospect of going alone or

44

being called a coward, Stan found a way out. He invited me along; and I was bribed not to tell Mum with the promise of a half-share in the tin of sweetened condensed milk that he had bought with his last pennies.

The only tin opener we possessed was a massive steel plunger with a wooden handle—too clumsy to be carried unobtrusively. So Stan waited until Mum had gone to feed the chickens, and opened the tin before we set off.

Entrusted not to spill the precious sticky contents of the tin, I followed Stan through the thickets and boggy sedges, surrounded by a buzzing cloud of sweet-toothed bluebottles, wasps and flies.

Just where the woods were thickest, and the path by the stream a green carpet beneath a tunnel of trees, I heard a rustling noise behind me. Stan heard it too. To restore our flagging courage we stopped for a taster from the tin.

Removing the two teaspoons that I had tucked up one knicker leg for easy transportation, I lifted back the half-opened lid. The one who took the biggest spoonful ate the most sticky-footed flies.

The rustling behind us materialised into Billy Wells, who had managed to slip away from his home unnoticed. He demanded at least one finger dip into our condensed milk tin. Or else he'd have his fish hooks back and tell our Mum.

Stan had brought along a dead shrew and a

hunk of bread pudding as fish bait, but I was despatched to hunt crawlies or small frogs to augment supplies.

Stan and Billy grumbled that I was frightening all the fish by moving about near them so I took myself off to the sunnier side of the weedy, dark, still pool.

No one knew how deep it was in the centre. An exploratory foot on the edge soon sank into glaucous mud, topped with decaying leaves.

A misshapen ash tree overhanging the murky water provided a comfortable perch in its double trunked fork. Up there, well away from the two fishermen, I could look down on coots and bad tempered moor hens, bustling their chicks in and out of the water. Mallard, shepherding families of ducklings, dabbled upending as they swam.

Rulers of the pool, and determined that the wildfowl should know it, a pair of mute swans glided on patrol. They were in the process of preparing a platform of twigs, reeds, and rushes, chivvying any waterfowl that came too near.

Below me, where the tree roots met the edge of the water, something that at first glance seemed to be a length of perished hosepipe, moved. A grass snake slid smoothly down into the murky depths.

Then, where the tree branches made dappled shadows on the water, I saw a sluggish movement just under the surface. As my eyes focused on the patch of sunlight, I noticed the long flat head and the enormous greenish-brown body of a fish. I had seen a smaller version of the same fish in a glass case at the gunsmith's where Dad bought his cartridges.

Forgetting caution, I called to Stan that I had seen a huge pike. Not that the boys took much notice. At that moment Billy was convinced that he had just caught a whale. When he landed a rusty old gramophone horn they gave up fishing in disgust and came around to join me.

Still as mice, we sat on the tree bough, watching and waiting, and, sure enough, the pike came back to its basking place again.

There was just one snag about dangling a baited hook down to tempt it. Stan had left the fishing gear on the far side of the pond.

As he slipped quietly down the tree trunk to get it the cob swan, preening his feathers on the bank beneath us, extended his enormous wings and stretched forth a flattened hissing head. He stamped his ungainly black webbed feet in irritation, and drove Stan back up the tree.

We were holed up there for hours, any attempt to move only producing a menacing display. Trying to humour it with stray lumps of the bread pudding Stan found in his pockets only seemed to make it more ferocious.

Suddenly, as if tiring of the pastime, the cob went back to his nest-building, and we scuttled back home.

To have mentioned the huge pike would have invited the business side of Mum's anger for going near Ladies Pool without her permission, and encouraged other would-be pike catchers up there too.

Instead, Billy and Stan slipped away to go fishing whenever they could, and the price of my silence was that I went too.

As the boys fished without success, I sat and watched the swans on their nest. One day when the eggs must have been almost due for hatching, we arrived at Ladies Pool to find the pen swan dead and half-submerged in the water, and no sign of the cob at all.

Rooks had already pecked most of the eggs in the nest, but Stan, risking his boots and a muddy bath, rescued one.

Carrying it home inside his shirt, he asked Mum if one of her broody hens could hatch it out. Mum put an end to our fishing trips to Ladies Pool, of course, but Stan's cygnet hatched and was kept as a tame pet for more than a year.

When its plumage had turned to white, Stan took the cygnet back to Ladies Pool and set it free.

The giant pike could be there still, and I like to think that one of the pair of majestic swans that still nest there is a descendant of the cygnet Stan raised all those years ago.

COUNTY WEDDING

'White dress in December?' Mum had never heard such pudding-headed nonsense.

'But Mum,' I pleaded, tearful, terribly afraid that of all the village school's sixty pupils, I alone might miss the opportunity of taking part in the most dramatic event in the district since the travelling knife-grinder was found dead in Stony Lane.

I repeated the schoolmaster's immutable orders.

'White dresses for the girls. All boys to wear shirts, ties, and no elbow-ragged jerseys. Grubby necks, faces or knees were to be scrubbed clean.'

Anyone not passing muster would be banished to mind the coats behind the yew trees in the graveyard on the north side of the church. Being a child with an inquisitive nature and not wanting to miss the once-in-a-lifetime occasion, I found that prospect truly appalling.

Besides, legend held that strange knocking noises were sometimes heard beneath one of the crumbly vault slabs on dark evenings—and I couldn't fathom out how departed spirits could know the difference between night and day. It would also mean walking over mounds where unbaptised babies were buried. To me, the thought of tiny souls who had never known the warmth of sunshine made it seem the saddest place on earth.

For all that we pupils comprehended, the schoolmaster's announcement about the celebrations might well have been in Russian, until my prosaic father explained.

High-flown phrases like 'celebrations appropriate to the nuptials of a fair scion of our aristocracy' were, he said, like 'the skin on a custard'.

Skimmed off, all it boiled down to was that Lordy's sister had hooked some poor fish and was landing him in her keep-net before he swam away.

Dad said her baited hook had dangled in deep water for so long that this wedding was a classic proof of the old saying 'Perseverance pays'. Mum, shushing, reminded him that little piglets had big ears.

So it was a grand wedding that all the fuss

was about. Light dawned at last. The Right Honourable Prudence was marrying a 'scion'. This, thanks to Dad's cryptic interpretation, I imagined to be some sort of king-sized aquatic creature. No wonder we village children were supposed to cheer along the route.

My parents' silver-edged wedding invitation took pride of place on our mantelpiece, propped up against the vase holding Dad's pipe-lighter spills. Surely then Mum must realise that pride took precedence over goose-pimples on so important an occasion.

I just had to conform to the schoolmaster's orders and wear a white frock.

Fidgeting under Mum's feet brought forth the compromise offer that if I churned the butter she would rummage through the Hope Chest to see what she could find. This wooden box looked like an over-enthusiastic corn bin. It was the size of a modern, chest-type deep freeze.

Anything outgrown or 'liable to come in useful' went into its cavernous depths where Mum found what seemed to her the ideal garment—my sister's confirmation dress.

My sister was well endowed in all the right places, and at least ten inches taller than I was, and bigger all round. Mum saw this as a definite advantage since it would enable me to wear layers of woollens underneath to keep out the cold.

The waist drooped near to my kneecaps, the

hemline hid my socks. As I stood churning the butter, Mum took a tacking-stitched tuck in the skirt.

'There,' she said. 'With paper flowers in your hair and something tied round your middle, you'll look a treat.'

The rigid curriculum of schoolwork had been abandoned for an orgy of crepe-paper rose-making, with all spare scraps cut into confetti petals. The boys were making 'wavers'—long streamers of coloured paper glued on to a rolled, cardboard wand.

Day after day the parson's sister rehearsed us in a choral tribute which we were to sing as the procession of gentry passed by. Some sharp, others flat, and all indifferent to the grievous musical harm we were rendering to the tune of Greensleeves, we chanted:

'Fair lady, humbly we beg we may
Bring glad tidings on this thy nuptial day.
We scatter roses along thy way
To bring comfort and joy to thy wedding.'

The Parson's sister also instructed us on how to curtsy to the aristocratic guests. These we would recognise instantly, since they would be wearing top hats and morning suits. That ruled out Dad. True, Old Humph the wagon-maker and undertaker had offered him the loan of his funeral topper. But when they removed the crepe band, the remainder looked moss green.

Mum revived the artificial flowers on her best hat with sugar water and curling tongs. Dressed in a moulting pony-skin coat that reeked of camphor, she looked one of the elite.

Albert Pearce, who pumped the church organ, was promised the unheard-of fee of five shillings, provided he kept the bellows full of wind.

The village postmistress reported that guests from The Hall had bought her entire stock of rice to throw over the bride.

The great day dawned cold but dry. Just before the ceremony we schoolchildren were assembled to line the churchyard path.

Paper roses in our hair, clutching bags full of paper petals, we curtsied and sang when we were told to, but were disappointed that among all the lords and ladies arriving, none wore a coronet or ermine gown. We had not caught one single glimpse of a scion fish either.

The bride arrived on the arm of His Lordship. According to the parson's sister, her wedding dress was an heirloom. It looked off-white and crumpled, as if it had been kept in our old Hope Chest, and it fitted worse than mine.

'Lordy' declared a school holiday and gave us all a sixpenny piece when the singing and flower-throwing was all over.

When the last of the guests had departed I helped Ethel Pearce and her affluent brother Albert to scrape up enough rice to fill our confetti bags.

With a few sultanas to disguise its dusty colour, they thought it would provide them with rice puddings for a week.

SLIPPY'S BOX

Bored in the isolation of the organ-blower's pew, Young Albert watched the Sunday morning sunshine stream through the stained glass windows of the church. Dust motes hung suspended in its rays, jewel-coloured patterns shimmered like a halo above the sexton's bowed and balding head.

'Some saint!' thought Albert, remembering how often the sanctimonious old fraud sampled the communion wine.

The parson, preaching to near-empty pews, droned on, hypnotically monotonous as a summer working bee. Behind a blue linen curtain Miss Minnie the lady organist lapsed into snatches of sleep.

Morning service always had a dreamlike air

about it to Albert. There was a subdued quality about sunlight inside the church, unreal and completely different from the brilliance of the morning beyond the thick, sound-muffling walls.

Outside, skylarks were soaring on upsurging winds. Prunus and primrose blossomed, lambs jumped for joy in the sunshine.

Inside the church the sun lacked warmth or strength serving only to intensify the stale smell of mildew and old hymn books.

The pattern of the sermon seldom varied. The sidesmen, shuffling upright in their pews, signified that they were preparing to do their rounds with the offertory plates. Albert gave the organ bellows a quick pump, knowing that this would wake Miss Minnie up.

Watching the indicator cord moving down as the bellows filled with air and up as they contracted, Albert pumped away at the handle. He was happy in the knowledge that once the final hymn was over he would soon be released from his duty, leaving six hours of glorious freedom before Evensong.

Those hours of Sunday freedom were not without interruptions. Albert's widowed mother kept the church clean and stoked the coke-burning stoves that heated it at weekends.

This often meant that just as Albert was wheeling his bike past the scullery window, prior to a quick dash to freedom, his mother would call out:

'Albert! Slip over and make sure they sullen old stoves ain't filling the place with fumes. And don't take a tribe of boys in with you, neither, or I'll know about it!'

She would too! Albert, conscious of being custodian of the massive key of the iron-banded door, set off along the footpath to the church very much alone.

At an age when, in a single sentence, his voice could alternate between a piping treble and a rumbling bass, Albert felt that he should be too grown-up to be nervous about going into an empty church. Nevertheless, he whistled loudly as he unlocked the heavy door. But the noise of the key on tumblers still echoed as he went through the porch and into the side chancel.

Sometimes high, sometimes low, but always with the full strength of his voice, Albert sang hymns as he hurried through his stoking duties, banging the iron poker on the stove lid, rattling the coke hod, anything to drown a silence so intense that it hung around him like an enveloping, icy cloak.

A yew bough cast moving shadows, tapping on a window; a bird fluttering and rustling in the belfry had the power to still all sound within his throat.

Not daring to look to left or right, much less behind him, Albert would top up the stoves, reset the dampers, then run down the aisles as fast as he could go, only starting to breathe normally again when the silence was locked safely behind the great oak doors.

Choir practice. Thursday, at seven sharp, and no excuses. The church was unheated, and, except for one solitary oil lamp near the organ, unlit.

Albert's cronies in the choir were within the pool of flickering light, but Albert sat in shadow, sharing the darkness of the top end of the side aisle with the carved recumbent figures of a medieval tomb.

The choirboys, catching his attention in the mirror fixed to the corner of the organ and angled so that Miss Minnie could signal when it was time to start pumping, pulled horror-struck faces and pointed to the darkness behind his back. If, as they said later, 'they old statues were a-moving', Albert was quite prepared to believe them.

Miss Minnie understood his nervousness, and on choir practice nights often popped her head around the curtain and rolled clandestine, curiously strong peppermints along the seat towards him. If they gained dust or fluff en route it didn't matter—they helped to keep the heebie-jeebies at bay.

If the organ wheezed more than usual, Slippy Springer, bell-ringer, grave-digger and parish poacher, would sometimes try to 'blow the months out of its innards', pumping frantically at the bellows as if he were drawing water from a deep-dug well.

One choir practice evening he came around the back of the organ to Albert, carrying a string-tied wooden box.

''Ere, young 'un, tuck this away under your pew for a day or two.'

Albert asked what the box contained.

'Something 'orrible,' Slippy answered. 'So don't you go getting nosy and trying to look.'

The longer Albert sat there the more curious he became, and when his friends in the choir asked what Slippy had wanted he told them about the box.

One boy with a flair for the macabre related something he had heard his father say.

'Dad reckons the churchyard is so crowded that when Slippy digs a grave he often finds someone else has been buried there first. I bet that old box is full of skulls and bones.'

'Tell you what, Albert. You try to get the string undone when you help your Mum clean the church on Saturday. Then we'll all have a quick look inside before Sunday morning service starts.'

Albert, hardly enthusiastic about the project, began his Saturday routine of filling oil lamps and lighting stoves. While his mother was busy cleaning the main part of the church Albert took his broom to the far end of the side-aisle, hoping against hope that the box behind the organ would be gone.

It wasn't. Albert gave it a tentative shove

with his broom. It moved a fraction, leaving its original position outlined on the floor in something red, congealed and suspiciously like blood.

His broom fell with a clatter as he shot off to find his mother. She cuffed him for being clumsy and asked if he imagined he'd seen a 'haunt'.

'Worse than that, Mum! Slippy Springer's gone and put a dead body in a box under my seat.' Not cursed with an over-vivid imagination, Albert's Mum said, 'Rubbish. Hold that dustpan still, then show me what you're yammering about.'

Convinced that his Mum was capable of dealing with bodies, bones or bogey-men, Albert followed her around behind the organ and watched her make short work of opening the box. Inside was a sack. This she lifted and turned upside down. Three brace of pheasants and a smelly hare fell on to the floor.

The personification of righteous anger, Albert's Mum confronted Slippy at his cottage door with the 'evidence', that dangled from the handlebars of Albert's bike.

'Dang all nosy, interfering women,' Slippy protested, 'Can't a man mind his own business in peace?'

'I'll *peace* you, you poacher,' Albert's Mum said, 'You get over to the church and clean that floor.'

AUNT FLO

My Aunt Florence imagined her mission in life to be the scourge of dirt and sin. Any sunlight that penetrated the tight-sealed windows of her terraced house was filtered by the starched lace curtains and half-drawn roller blinds.

The massive Maidenhair fern that provided cover for Aunt Flo to watch the wickedness of the city unobserved, knew better than to shed its leaves. And every hard-seated chair stood upright and straight-backed, reflected in the skating rink surface of the waxed linoleum floors.

Armed with bucket, mop and broom, Aunt Flo engaged in a never-ending battle to keep the devil Dirt beyond her hearthstoned doorstep. Nevertheless she regarded it as a family obligation to come and stay with us on the farm once or twice a year.

This duty she undertook with all the *joie-de-vivre* of a martyr suffering the penance of walking in boots full of dried peas. She detested the isolation of the countryside since it provided so many opportunities to sin in secret. By her standards it was nothing more than field upon field, all filled with dirt.

Her visits usually coincided either with the height of the fruit-picking season or those last few hectic weeks before Christmas, when we were preparing table poultry to be sold.

It always fell to my lot to meet her off the Saturday morning bus at Lockley Bottoms.

We would trudge back up the hill, with Aunt Flo dressed in funeral black, darting ahead like a skinny, wing-flapping crow, while I carried a heavy Gladstone bag in one hand and an enormous empty wicker basket in the other.

This hamper was known as 'Aunt Flo's Harvest Home', for until she had 'safely gathered in' all that she could acquire for nothing there was little hope of her going back home.

If I appeared to lag too far behind, my Aunt would stop and delve into her handbag. It was not to offer me a sweet, because sweets were to her just 'gratification of the flesh'. Instead, she handed out mind-improving tracts.

Encouraged by phrases like 'Lo, they shall be cast down into the pit', I matched her pace in my anxiety to hand her over to Mum.

Aunt Flo took precautions against country contamination by bringing tins of Keatings Insect Powder with her. For she was convinced that every farm animal had 'creatures', making anyone that came into contact with them suspect, too.

She scattered insect powder around her like talc, and the aura of red pepper and pyrethrum in which she moved sent the kitchen cats scuttling for the back door whenever she appeared.

Tins of flea powder appeared in the most unexpected places. On one occasion I was so engrossed in Aunt Flo's account of a high-class funeral tea she had attended that I seasoned the steak and kidney pudding I was preparing with flea powder instead of pepper and salt.

My father had commented on the odd taste of the meal when realisation dawned. While we watched anxiously for medical reactions, Aunt Flo hunted in her handbag for an appropriate text.

Funerals were Aunt Flo's forte, and many a bereaved family in the city must have been puzzled by the unfamiliar, dark-clad little woman among the mourning cortège.

If she happened to be asked back to the funeral tea, she made herself useful by handing round ham sandwiches, discussing the dear departed's chances of escaping everlasting purgatory, and doing the washing up.

If she noticed signs of the demon Dirt in her host's kitchen, she tackled that as well.

A ride in a taxi and the opportunity to distribute a few uplifting texts, plus a good tea, made Aunt Flo feel that life was indeed worthwhile.

It seemed a pretty ghoulish pastime, and while my parents agreed that she was certainly different, they maintained that under all the acid layers was a lonely, well-intentioned soul.

Unconvinced, I thought that peeled to the pith, Aunt Flo would still emerge as a sour lemon underneath. I was as pleased as she when her 'Harvest Home' hamper was full and I could wave her goodbye as I saw her off on the bus.

That was in the early part of the war and what with being short-handed on the farm, and the village a reception zone for evacuees, we had little time to worry overmuch about Aunt Flo, until we received a telegram containing only one word.

'BOMBED!' Aunt Flo, who loathed the country, decided she would come and live with us.

Dad and I took a wagon to the city to collect what could be salvaged from her home. It was difficult to determine where the houses ended and the street began, for the blast had ripped out the front walls and the slate-less roofs stood open to the sky.

Amid the rubble stood Aunt Flo, driving the

civil defence demolition unit to despair. Where her unfortunate neighbours had left their unsafe houses, with the unmade beds and tumbled furniture open to the public gaze, Aunt Flo had shoved, heaved and pushed all that was moveable into the comparative shelter of the three remaining upright walls of her front room, and was standing on guard outside.

She noticed the remnants of her Maidenhair fern entwining a leaning lamp-post as she clambered into the wagon, and prophesied that there would be a judgement on that Hitler fellow for making so much dust.

As I washed the soot and powdered glass from her hair she looked far less austere, as if the first layer of her sourness had been peeled off.

Each day she disappeared into her room where her furniture was stored, polishing and dusting, preparing for the day when providence would provide her with a roof of her own again.

Providence came in the form of a dairyman from the next village who was at our place buying fodder for his herd.

Like us, he was short-handed, but while we could get by with seasonal labour, he needed someone reliable to do dairy work every day. There was an empty farm cottage waiting for a dairy hand.

Aunt Flo may not have known the front end

65

of a cow from the back, but she did know how to keep things clean, so once again we loaded the wagon with her belongings, and set off for the cottage at Pork Green.

She didn't live there long, for within six months she had married her employer, on the principle that it was sinful waste to have two kitchen fires burning instead of one.

With her zeal for work the dairy flourished. Although she was never exactly frivolous, one often heard her singing as she sterilised and polished dairy pans.

She died a rich woman, leaving all her cash to a charity for fallen women. And she left me a legacy, a text which read; 'Virtue is its own reward'.

THE CREATURE IN THE WOOD

Walt said that folks could think as they liked. He had been a forestry worker, man and boy, for over thirty years and when he told them that there was something mighty peculiar prowling around in Church Woods he wasn't talking just to give exercise to his tongue.

He flatly denied the suggestion that it was just a fanciful notion, imagined after a darts match at the Hare and Hounds. In fact he took offence.

'Takes more than a few pints of bitter to make me hear some creature breathing heavily in the furze and bracken along Newtake Track or see young chestnut branches still swaying where some powerful great beast had just blundered through.'

Walt went to work with some reluctance. He admitted to Old Bailey, his fellow wood-cutter, it needed more courage to stay at home and face his wife's accusations of 'lead swinging' than face unknown creatures lurking in the forest.

They went to work their separate ways where the forest tracks divided. A couple of days later Old Bailey confessed to Walt that he, too, had heard the sound of dead twigs snapping in the wood behind him and had experienced the feeling that he was being watched.

Without mentioning the fact to anyone else, for fear of being classed as a pair of 'bogging old wimmin', they decided they would be easier in their minds if they worked within hailing distance of each other.

Establishing a habit of eating their 'bait' together at midday, they sat under an oak tree with their customary bread, cheese and onion, and leaning against the tree trunk began to doze.

A rustling in the undergrowth close by instantly roused Old Bailey, who jumped up and flung his axe towards the moving bushes. His shouts mingled with an unearthly high-pitched squeal. As Walt, now fully awakened, watched the shaking and quivering bushes both men, considerably shaken, compared notes on what they had heard and seen.

Within an hour of their home-going the

entire village was aware that some sort of screaming, beady-eyed, pale-faced manifestation had been lurking near Old Bailey, who had tried to cleave it with his axe. They also knew that Walt had definitely confirmed that something pale and huge and squealing had vanished into the brushwood near the oak tree at Newtake Fork.

Beneath the surface of any rural community, a thousand years of superstitions and half-remembered old beliefs lie dormant. All sorts of explanations for the apparition were put forward, from witchcraft, sorcery and black magic, to the schoolmaster's conviction that what the woodmen had heard was the mating call of an albino fox.

That theory was soon disposed of for as the two men said, foxes, albino or not, have fur, and from the one glimpse they'd had of their 'creature', all that they could see was skin.

The death of any old broiler fowl came to be regarded as uncanny. A day of continuous thunder and lightning, when all the milk yield at Chapple's dairy went sour, was questioned as being the work of witches, too.

Dogs and cats that had been missing for ages, strayed sheep, and the plump porker that Charlie Cartwright's commonsense told him had disappeared from its sty to provide, as he said, 'some thieving varmints' dinners', were now remembered and thought to have become victims of that unknown creature stalking in the woods.

The parson, trying to keep some sort of hold over the situation, gave some soul-shriving sermons of the bell, book, and candle variety. These were lost on almost empty pews because the more agile of his congregation had joined the lads of the village in a new Sunday pastime, hunting for the creature in Church Woods.

Armed with cudgels and a variety of guns that were potentially more dangerous than any lurking beastie, the searchers started off enthusiastically. But after a few weeks fruitless hunting, they soon lost heart.

The woods were vast, with stretches of untamed, almost impenetrable undergrowth alternating with tracts of thick chestnut underwood.

Walt and Old Bailey were branded as a pair of scarifying jokers that deserved to be ducked in the village pond.

During the rest of that summer the tales of strange creatures and weird happenings died down.

But one Sunday evening a farmhand from Foxley brought his hysterical and trembling wife into the tap-room of the Hare and Hounds.

They had been gathering hazel nuts along Newtake path when something small and pink had shot off through the undergrowth just in front of the tree where the unfortunate woman was nutting, and had disappeared from sight.

'T'was like a naked babby that I glimpsed scuttling away from me. And when I bawled out to Thomas, we could both hear several of the objects scampering away'.

'May the saints preserve us', said the landlord, giving her a drink for nothing, which was unheard of. 'Walt's beast has gone and spawned a crowd of young 'uns in the wood.'

Walt and Old Bailey, now feeling completely vindicated, thought it their duty as woodmen to take more drastic action. Since the oak at Newtake Fork was the scene of their first sighting, they decided to climb up and keep watch from it, staying all night if needs be. Someone, somehow, had to find out what sort of creature was breeding in the wood.

It was dusk when Walt heard grunting in the distance.

'Listen,' he nudged Old Bailey, 'Them things is trying to talk!'

There was a good deal of thrashing about in the cover on the far side of the pathway, then a huge sow and ten piglets emerged and began snuffling for acorns underneath the tree.

The men climbed down on stiff and trembling legs, only to scramble up again to escape the infuriated sow that promptly charged at them.

It took several weeks before a properly organised search party of beaters worked through the woods, and eventually the pigs broke cover out into Humpty Dumpty

71

Meadow.

They were driven into the sheep-dipping compound in one corner, but left it splintered like matchwood in their efforts to escape.

When they were eventually captured Charlie Cartwright, identifying the sow as his lost porker by her ear tag, tried to keep them in his pig pounds. But they refused to eat pig swill, rooting up and smashing everything around.

There was only one course of action for their owner. The young porkers were sold to the butcher, while the old sow provided Walt, Old Bailey, and the rest of the pig hunters with some mighty tough Sunday joints of meat.

THE SCHOOL OAK

The Mid-Victorian builders of the old schoolroom designed it so that sheer enjoyment of the surroundings would never distract future pupils from their work. The windows were narrow, high and few.

Lack of natural light and dark, dull, painted brickwork condemned generations of village children to peer at slate or book in perpetual twilight during the months of winter. All looked forward to the traditional acknowledgement that it was summer when both the inner and outer doors of the schoolroom would be wedged back and opened wide.

Those fortunate and brainy enough to sit in the two front rows of top division were offered a tantalising glimpse of the playground through the narrow windowless lobby with its stone floor, broken coat-pegs, row of chipped and stained enamel mugs and constantly dripping tap.

For the rest, blue summer skies seen through the thick distorted panes of high, never-opened windows became dusty diamond-shapes of bottle green.

Nothing else was visible beyond the classroom walls unless one was considered dim enough to be relegated to 'dunce's corner' right against the back wall. I earned that distinction by informing a visiting inspector that Madame Guillotine was a French woman who lost her head.

Pressed further to describe the French method of execution, I described what had always appeared to me to be a sharpened hay knife rolling the aristocratic heads off as neatly as mangolds being tossed into a basket at wurzel-clamping time.

By sitting straight-backed and on the far edge of the dunce's seat I found that I could see the trunk and topmost branches of a tree that Old Bailey, the woodman, estimated to have been between three and four hundred years old.

It was known to all and sundry as School Oak and history that had hitherto been just a dry-as-dust jumble of unremembered people waging unnecessary battles in unpronounceable places, was latched on to my memory by relating the size that the oak tree must have been with the time when the historical events took place.

The playground proper was just a dusty patch of knee-lacerating gravel with a strip of grass and a shallow ditch dividing it from School Lane. Dominating grass and gravel School Oak stood majestic at the far end of the grass. In high summer we 'dinner children' were allowed to eat our jam sandwich dinners in its shade.

Schoolboys carved their initials into its bark; girls made acorn necklaces. The biggest lads, climbing to the topmost dying branches, boasted that they could see the ocean, Lockley Church spire, America, a woodpecker's nest, or the old schoolmaster's 'Missus' up in School House front bedroom changing her drawers.

Monkey-like, we hung to it with our feet off the ground, made skipping rope swings on the lower branches and, giggling, wondered which of our respective older brothers or sisters had made public their intentions towards their sweethearts by marking its trunk with a white, painted kiss.

None of us realised that the cross on the bark was the old tree's kiss of death until we heard the scrunch of hobnailed boots on the playground gravel and saw Old Bailey and Tom Saffron standing in the schoolroom doorway.

Lessons ceased abruptly for all and we were marched outside. Habit made the leaders head toward the oak tree, but we were sent back in the opposite direction, with the master ordering us, 'Back! Back farther!'

In between unwrapping a cross-cut saw from its sacking cover and laying out wedges and axe, Old Bailey conducted a running argument with the schoolmaster.

His boss had sent him to fell a tree, not to entertain a parcel of young varmints hustled out of school. He had felled more acres of timber than the schoolmaster had seen hot dinners, and when he felled a tree it laid where it was told. All he had said was that one awkward branch would land three feet from the schoolroom door and there was no need to get into a muck-sweat about that.

Nevertheless we sat in the sunshine watching Old Bailey swing an axe with arms that were whipcord and old leather. The cross-cut saw sang through the wood until it struck a knot. It seemed as though the tree was screaming in agony. Suddenly it was as if we were reluctantly watching a public execution.

I tried to warn the master about the nuthatch fledglings in the hole at the top of the trunk, but was told that this was Nature Study and to be quiet and sit down.

The tree trembled and shivered; then, like a dying man drawing one last sighing breath as he falls into oblivion, it toppled to the ground in a crash of flying bark and splintered broken limbs.

School Lane and the old schoolroom looked shabbier, smaller and uninteresting. There were few of us that did not wish we had the strength and power to put the tree back upright and make the school playground as it was before.

Nature Study became a woodwork lesson as the pupils were detailed to collect all the smaller broken branches and stack them beside the woodshed in the schoolmaster's garden. Old Bailey and Tom Saffron began sawing the main branches from the trunk.

By now it was 'all go home' time, but I stayed on because the three-horse timber wagon arriving from Jeffery's woodyard was followed by Father leading Ginger, our cantankerous but extremely powerful Suffolk Punch.

Blocks and pulleys were hung on to shear-legs above the stripped tree trunk. Its girth made the men around it seem very puny and I marvelled that its weight could be lifted high off the ground by two steady, patient horses gently pulling on a rope.

The timber wagon was backed into position underneath and as the trunk was lowered on to it, it looked like a fat old lady perched on top of a baby's pram.

The size and length of it would create problems along the five-mile journey through the lanes. I knew that I would be allowed to watch its progress providing that I stayed well to the rear. In fact, I was welcome as a useful messenger if help was needed or anything went wrong.

All went well until it was within a hundred feet of the timber yard gateway. Then the back bolster of the wagon gave way, making the back axle bend ominously and the iron-shod wooden wheels tilt in. I was sent running to fetch 'Old Humph', the wheelwright and wagon builder, because the load was too dangerous to move and too dangerous to leave where it stood.

Under Humph's directions the wagon was shored up so the trunk could be sawn into lengths in situ. As the men around him worked, Old Humph examined what remained of the old School Oak.

''Tis beautiful', he told Mr Jeffery, who was more concerned about his damaged wagon.

'I'll do a deal,' Old Humph went on. 'Give me that seven-foot length and I'll repair the timber tug for nothing but a pint or two. Seasoned properly that bit of oak 'ud make as fine a coffin as any man could wish for.'

'Make another one for me from the length cut off next to it and I'll agree,' Mr Jeffery said.

So the two baulks of timber were unloaded by the roadside, 'seasoning' until Old Humph could find time to make them into the old men's last earthly homes. He never did, for both went in a hard winter of deep frost and

Asian flu.

The old timber yard and the sheds where men made hurdle gates is now a garden centre. The new road has caused the entrance to be altered, but on the edge of the customers' car park, surrounded by concrete toadstools, plastic pixies and plaster toads the two pieces of trunk lie, sound as the day when Old Bailey felled School Oak.

THE CORN DOLLY

Dad believed that feeding corn into a thresher was an agrarian version of playing the fruit machines. The difference was that one swallowed corn while the other swallowed coins. In both cases luck was needed if a man was to make a profit or just break even. Equally both could leave him flat broke.

Heartbreak and tail corn had emerged from the threshing machine for several seasons, but one year Dad stood by the corn chute knowing that for once in our farming lives we had hit the jackpot.

Watching a steady cascade of Archer barley overflow his cupped hands to fill sack upon sack, he realised that the tally chalked up on a wooden guard board showed that the ratio of corn threshed to acreage planted would average well over a ton an acre.

Top malting barley realised the highest prices. Samples of this merchandise would not be hawked round the dealers like feed corn—in blue paper sugar bags.

When it grew too dark to work out of doors we made white cotton sample bags. We sewed them by lamplight, on a machine that had tackled everything from wedding veils to mending corn sacks since before Queen Victoria's Diamond Jubilee.

White sample bags would emphasise the dust-free golden quality of the grain when it was offered direct to the brewers in the city.

It was mid-day when the belts and drums stopped turning. By mid-afternoon the yard was empty. The great door of the barn stood opening onto silence.

The only unthreshed corn left inside were the few traditionally tied sheaves saved to decorate the church at Harvest Festival. But the last sheaf that had been cut hung from a beam on a length of binder twine, out of reach of the rats, to await the arrival of my uncle.

Uncle George would fashion it into a corn dolly. When it was finished he would hang it on a special hook over the fireplace on beams of the kitchen ceiling. There it would stay until it was replanted when the next spring-sowing season began.

We did not realise that we were following a

pagan ritual, based on the belief that the Earth Spirit took refuge in the last stalks of standing corn at harvest time and must be returned to wake all growing things in spring.

Twisting corn stalks into shapes and patterns was a pastime that my great-grandfather had taught to his grandson. Now Uncle George was keeping touch with the background whence he sprang.

The dolly hung all winter gathering smoke and spiders, and if my Mum grumbled about the dusty old thing, it was not fear of upsetting the spirits that prevented her throwing it out.

Uncle George had the local reputation of being a rare boy-o. It was easy to upset his contrary temperament. He could be generous and jovial, or as cussed as they come.

We thought him to be frightfully rich and important since the status of his city employment allowed him to have two weeks holiday a year, one of them with pay.

More than that, he and Aunt Ella lived in a suburban villa where hot water came out of taps. For a short while the stable under the walnut tree in their garden had actually garaged Uncle's car.

Being among the elite had its drawbacks, for Uncle tended to forget that his Austin Seven needed refuelling and he was frequently stranded miles from home. Eventually it ran out of petrol by an isolated farm gate, and Uncle left it because he 'couldn't abide an object that stopped dead as soon as it thought it was thirsty'. The farmer he left it with drove it around for years. Uncle's car was replaced by a pony and cart, in which he would bring Aunt Ella to visit us twice a year.

Dad took stock of the sacks of corn stacked in the barn, where the last sheaf swung from the beam. The hard work and pressure of threshing time had slackened off.

Not for long though. For as we shut the door of our corn store we heard the clipped trot of a high-stepping pony and saw Uncle George and Aunt Ella driving down the lane.

Mum welcomed them while I did a rush job on a bedroom that had not seen broom or duster since threshing began. The goose-feather mattress, kept permanently aired in the cupboard by the chimney, was hauled out on to the bedstead. All was made ready and I was back in the kitchen before our visitors began their second cup of tea.

Uncle was enthusiastic about the samples of barley and volunteered to drive Dad into town to try and sell it the following day. After a damp kiss from Aunt Ella, I asked Uncle George how things were going.

'Well girl, there's a lot of truth in the saying, "A woman, a dog and a walnut tree, the more you beats 'em the better they be". Your Aunt is flourishing, the walnut tree is loaded, and the pup comes at a gallop when I call. The only trouble with beating 'em is that my right arm fair gives me the agonies with overwork.'

Uncle made the corn dolly that evening and early the following morning Dad and Uncle set off into town. Given time to sell the corn and rest the pony, they should have been back soon after lunch.

Aunt Ella settled herself in the armchair by the kitchen fire while Mum churned butter. Both women, glad of each other's company, enjoyed a bit of female chat.

I was too busy with the outdoor jobs to join them and by afternoon milking time was hopefully listening for the sound of pony hooves. The sow that chose that afternoon to farrow seemed determined to crush or eat her new-born piglets in the sty.

The ordinary routine became disorganised. I was still racking up and watering the horses as it grew dark.

By now both Mum and Aunt Ella were convinced that their husbands had been murdered for the barley money, or had landed in a ditch. To calm their anxiety I volunteered to cycle as far as High Common, and if the men were not on the road, to alert the village policeman on the way back.

It was hazy with mist up on the common. At first I thought I heard a moorland pony ambling up the road; then I heard iron-shod wheels on gravel and saw Uncle's pony walking with its head down below the level of the shafts. Dad was leading it, and it seemed to be pulling a great weight. The cart was piled high with boxes and from somewhere among them I could hear Uncle's throat-rending snores.

Convinced by Dad that there was no need to worry, I rode back to tell Mum and my Aunt the good news that their husbands would soon be home.

When they reached the yard I helped Dad unload box after box of apples, which mystified me, seeing that our crop was still waiting to be picked off the trees.

Dad, explaining their delay, said that while he was at the brewery offices, Uncle George had called first at the Market Tavern, then at the market itself. It was while he was trying to attract Dad's attention by waving, that he inadvertently bid for three, ten-bushel lots of sour apples.

'Yes', said Uncle, sobering up with every minute. 'Then I got to thinking. It cost me sixpence for a pint of cider in the Market Tavern, and 30 bushels of crushed apples would make a lot of juice. It only needed something to crush them, and I've found a heavy old mangle going cheap. When I go back to collect it tomorrow, I'll show you how cider should be made.'

Mum and Dad smiled at each other. The profit on the malting barley meant a healthy bank balance, and if old George wanted to spend his holiday mangling apples, he might even make a fair sample of cider at that.

The corn dolly swung above the hearth, and the Earth Spirit sheltered safely in the old house to await the spring.

THE DUMMY

He sat in the draughtiest corner of the schoolroom, a 'big' boy in the 'babies' class, as out of place as a turnip in a radish row. Too large to tuck his knees beneath his desk, he sat sideways—blocking the gangway with his enormous studded boots, into which sagging socks subsided.

His trousers, an indecisive cross between 'long 'uns' cut too short, or shorts that were too long, ended baggy-legged around his calves. There was a gap between his breeches and his shrunken jersey, the sleeves of which had long lost contact with his wrists.

This made him look as if his lower half had no connection with his top, as if some ill-disposed toy-maker had wrongly assembled two halves from different-sized marionettes.

To the schoolmarm he was an illiterate vexatious nuisance, ignoring every other activity in the schoolroom to sit drawing confused pictures on his slate.

The tightly clutched pencil, incessantly scraping and screeching across his slate, set her teeth on edge and got on her nerves to the extent that she was continually bellowing 'Will-Yum!' at the top of her powerful voice. 'Will-Yum' would continue engrossed and unheeding until the stinging weight of her hand, making contact with his ears, penetrated his mute world.

To his fellow pupils he was 'The Dummy', an oddity who hid his face behind the drooping peak of a 'cheese-cutter' cap, made to fit his head by virtue of an enormous tuck stitched in the back.

He lived on the far side of Penny-Pot Woods, a three-mile walk from school. Lacking contact with his fellows, Will Yum developed some instinct for taming a menagerie of small wild animals. This created mayhem in the classroom, for he was liable to dive into the pockets of his voluminous breeches and extract a grass snake, a dormouse, or a rat.

Unwanted kittens and orphaned rabbits found their way into Will Yum's pockets and he would set off home with a rapturous expression on his face and a cocoa tin in his hand. This he used to supplement the diet of his pets, slipping surreptitiously through a hedge to milk one of the grazing cows, until the tin was full.

Work was short when Will Yum left school. He became more elusive, shunning his fellow men. One might see him petting some savage chain-bound farm dog or find him stroking an old horse turned out to graze.

Undeniably, he had a way with animals, but local farmers reasoned that a half-wit who recognised no danger was a menace to himself, was unemployable, and certainly not to be encouraged near stock.

One depressing winter, when Dad was struck down by illness, and our financial circumstances were far from good, I was ploughing Twelve Acre field with Jim, the chestnut horse, and Punch, the grey.

We had plodded up and down the furrows all finger-freezing morning long when I saw Mum coming across the rough stubble with my lunch; a jug of cocoa, the top of an oven-warm cottage-loaf and a hunk of cheese.

Leaving the horses standing at the end of the furrow I went to meet her. I returned to find Will Yum, who stood wiping Jim's flank with his old cap.

Mum's new-baked bread smelled delicious, which was probably why he stood hesitantly watching. I broke it in half and offered him a portion with a lump of cheese. Solemnly he

89

accepted it, and equally solemnly divided his share into three, giving one piece to Jim, one to Punch, and eating the last piece himself.

I think that was when I was absolutely certain that great as Will Yum's affliction was, he was definitely not 'daft'.

All afternoon he walked up and down as I ploughed, first tentatively fingering the reins, then actually using them to control the horses, so that I could concentrate on holding the plough.

For the first time that I could remember Will Yum's eyes were bright with laughter.

Sometimes weeks would go past without Will Yum coming near our farm, but as he grew confident that no one there would mock or hurt him, he would materialise out of nowhere and we would find him grooming the horses, or cleaning out the cowshed.

Mum fed him chunks of bread pudding; Dad encouraged him in simple tasks, communicating by chalking illustrative sketches on the top of the corn bin.

Winter and a humid summer passed.

Then farmer after farmer watched a season's work and his cattle's feed go up in smoke. The rash of stack fires followed a pattern, and suspicions of arson gathered strength.

Dad gave this no credence, but knowing that the loss of our crop would break us, used the stack boring iron to ventilate the ricks. The cores of extracted hay were extremely warm.

At a neighbouring farm, the stack-yard was beside the thatched stables and barn, and when the farmer was awakened by shouting and the sound of whinnying horses, he feared the worst.

He found one stack blazing, the stables full of smoke. But the horses, minus their stable halters, were safely turned out in the field. Whoever had rescued them had vanished into the night.

Word went round that Will Yum's jacket and boots had been singed by the fire. Convinced that his son was guilty, his father had decided to have Will Yum put away in an institution.

Dad was equally convinced that the fires had been caused by spontaneous combustion. If Will Yum was involved at all, it was more likely he had released our neighbour's stock. This was entirely discounted. The rescuer had shouted. Will Yum could not speak.

To reassure himself Dad decided to visit the institution to which Will Yum had been sent. The transformation was remarkable. For the first time in his life he was warmly clad and adequately fed. A hearing aid had brought him unimagined sounds, and therapy was encouraging noises from his throat.

Best of all he was free to wander around the grounds and there was an endless supply of paper for drawing pictures. He could tear it, sheet after sheet from a toilet roll, whenever he chose.

Gentle Will Yum had found a paradise on earth.

THE MUTUAL BROTHERS

The Mutual Brotherhood Club at the Hare and Hounds began in the days when sickness meant no pay and a farm worker's idea of Utopia was the entitlement to 'Eight hours work, eight hours play, eight hours sleep and eight shillings a day'.

For sixpence a week a wage earner could ensure that if illness brought the wolf of poverty slavering around his door, the few shillings of the 'Mutual' allowance helped to keep it at bay.

Membership had the added advantage of providing a wife-proof excuse for a weekly visit to the Hare and Hounds each subscription night.

Fully paid-up members fortunate enough to

have had no recourse to sick benefit during the year shared what was in the kitty each December and, thanks to the business acumen of the landlord, often drew out far more than they put in.

A lot of buying and selling swelled the funds; at one time everyone in the village without pigs or poultry of their own saved their scraps to feed the 'Mutual' porkers fattening in sties in the pub's back yard.

Most of the geese that cropped the grass on the village green belonged to the 'Mutual', and the united wrath of the village would descend on any catapult-carrying lad caught 'flustering off their fat'.

Mid-January brought the opportunity for old and new members to join for the following year, with few men in the district failing to take advantage of our rural self-help scheme.

They were actively encouraged by the local farmers and landowners, who contributed ham, baked potatoes, bread, cheese and cider, to turn 'joining night' at the Hare and Hounds into a social event.

The customers crammed into the bar on those nights numbered far more than the usual patronage during the slack winter season.

Ladies were actively discouraged at the Hare and Hounds so that all the members of the Mutual Brotherhood were male, but one.

The exception was a widow, a lady of unquestionable character and strength. Any shy and gentle characteristics that caused her to be named Violet in infancy, wilted as she matured, for in no way could she be said to 'bloom unseen'.

Booted, gaitered, dressed in whipcord breeches and a donkey jacket that had faded to a shade of lichen green, she could carry corn sacks with the men and reduce other field-working women to tears as they tried to keep up with her pace of work.

At root harvest, the wurzels that she pulled would fly like missiles into heaps, and anyone invoking the rough side of her temper was liable to find a mangold hurtling at his head.

Cricket enthusiasts often expressed regret that as a female, Violet was debarred from participating in a game in which her speed and accuracy of throwing would have qualified her for the county team at least.

As cuddly and yielding as a gorse bush, Violet was the sole representative of her sex on 'joining nights' at the Hare and Hounds and as such, took good care that no mere man made coarse remarks in her hearing. If they did Violet would adjust the woolly beret that seemed to have become part of her head and, with scant ceremony, lift the offender like a sack of potatoes to deposit him in the pig sties in the yard.

One year, when the cider sent down from Four Oaks Farm seemed more potent than any previous brew, the new hand who had been responsible for its improvement came down to the inn to join the 'Mutual' scheme.

Rumour had it that he came originally from Devon, but nothing was known about his background. If he had a surname no one heard him use it, and to the people in our community, he was known as 'Johnno Jack'.

As befitted a newcomer he went early, sat quiet, and bought more ale than he was offered.

While the evening was still young he left to relieve the horseman up at Four Oaks, who was keeping watch over a sick mare, and to give him the opportunity to add his name to the 'Mutual Brotherhood' lists.

By custom, just before closing time, when the meeting was ending in an alcoholic haze, the landlord would read out a list of the members to ensure that all who wanted to participate had joined.

It was at this point that someone realised that the Four Oaks horseman had not 'signed on', nor had Johnno Jack come back.

The farm foreman risked parting with the inaugural joining fee of one shilling in the horseman's name, but everyone wondered why neither man was there for what rated, by our standards, as a big night in the year.

The cold clammy darkness of a drizzling winter night met the home-going 'Brotherhood' like a black woollen blanket as they passed beyond the pub doorway into the night.

Violet strode off ahead of the group of men whose homeward steps would lead them past her cottage. The 'Brotherhood', somewhat the worse for wear, relied on the carriage lamp that 'Post Hole Willy' carried and his uncanny ability to steer a straight course home.

Violet was safely home with the tight-drawn blind of her bedroom window reflecting flickering candle-light before the 'Mutual Brothers' wavered their way along the lane.

One, more daring or more drunk than the rest of his fellows, began to serenade her with 'Goodnight Sweetheart' and all stood stock still waiting for the tirade that would follow if Violet took offence.

In the silence, someone heard a groan that seemed to come from a deep ditch on the opposite side of the lane.

The groaning grew louder and more agonised—Post Hole Willy, pushed to the front by the others because he held the lamp, and because they were more scared than he, peered over and saw Johnno Jack, plastered in mud and stagnant water, lying helpless in the ditch.

'He reckons he's busted his leg. Any road, he can't get out of the dyke.'

One of the party recalled that when his horse broke a leg they had to shoot it. Someone else suggested they should search for a hurdle gate to carry him home. With a strength derived from desperation, Johnno Jack bawled at them to get him out somehow.

Still wearing beret and boots, with her donkey jacket over a voluminous calico nightdress, Violet came striding out of her gate, intent on denting a few drunken heads.

'Great stupid lummocks!' she called them, as she clambered down into the ditch and hauled Johnno Jack out.

Rejecting all offers of help she carried him like a baby into the cottage and slammed the door.

Using a broomstick and her gaiters, Violet splinted Johnno's injured leg and cleaned him up in much the same way as one would groom a plough horse that had floundered in the mud.

In the clearer-headed light of morning Will and the 'Mutual Brothers' decided that the doctor ought to call at Violet's cottage. There he found that apart from an injured limb there were no other physical after-effects of Johnno's mishap.

At first Johnno revelled in the luxury of a feather mattress and coilsprung softness of Violet's best-room bed. She would not hear of him being moved until he was better and even argued his case when he claimed sickness allowance from the 'Mutual Brotherhood' scheme.

She took his mud-stained clothes away and washed them, but after a week Johnno became restless and suggested he might return to the two-roomed wooden hut he called his home. This let loose a flood of indignation. Had Violet not compromised her good name to offer him shelter? There was talk in the village, and scandalising tongues would only be stilled if he offered her his name.

She happened to be holding a billhook in one hand, and a poker in the other at the moment she proposed marriage. Since there is nothing more vulnerable than a man in his predecessor's night-shirt, Johnno consented to become Violet's husband number two.

Violet thought it was a pleasant gesture when Johnno offered to buy a memorial stone for her first husband's grave. She was not so happy when it was erected, for the inscription described the deceased as being 'set free from a life of long and continuous suffering, bravely borne'! Everyone knew that Violet's first had not suffered any long illness—but had departed this life suddenly.

She took the message on the gravestone in the spirit that it was meant. Johnno took himself back to his hermit's life in the wooden shack among the cider apple trees in Four Oaks orchard. At apple picking time, Violet would be there hurling a fusillade of rotting fruit at her estranged husband's door.

Now the 'Mutual Brotherhood' is disbanded, but under the old gnarled trees in Four Oaks orchard there are still small bright red apples lying amid the tussocks of old grass.

PAINTBRUSH

Silent as her own shadow, the old vixen emerged from the ebony blackness of the spinney to cross the moonlit orchard. The night breeze blowing cool upon her greying muzzle reassured her that she was up-wind of any danger.

Amidst the falling apple blossom, she slipped from one tree-shaded pool of darkness to the next.

As she ran cautiously along the ditch behind the back garden fences, a growling, grumbling dog warned her that he knew just where she was. Prone, with belly flattened to the ground, she immediately became part of the dark dampness of the ditch.

An upstairs window suddenly became an

illuminated square, an irritable human voice demanded silence, then all was quiet.

The last few defiant yaps had the muffled resonance of a dog incarcerated behind brick walls and wooden doors. Realising that she was comparatively safe, the vixen hurried on.

She was old, her cubs were hungry, and her milk had almost gone. The mallard that had been yesterday's breakfast for her four youngsters had nowhere near satisfied their needs.

Relentless maternal instinct urged her onward, past the forge yard wall and out into the village street.

Parked cars, strange shapes in the darkness, stinking of oil fumes, seemed totally unconnected with the scent of her worst enemy—Man.

Beyond the skirting trees, the grass of the village green afforded her no cover. Slinking forward, the vixen made no sound to disturb shelducks and mallard slumbering close by the rush-rimmed pond.

Water-fowl were not her objective. Amid the reeds, where sedge and pondweed mingled, a pair of migratory Canada geese were sleeping side by side. One leap, timed carefully, could fell one of them, providing food in plenty for her half-starved cubs.

The vixen lifted her head to sniff the wind and, tensing her muscles, sprang. An explosion of searing heat and pain convulsed her before she dropped down into oblivion.

The men who had spent cold, car-bound hours of waiting, congratulated themselves on having shot the marauder that had been threatening the wild-fowl of the pond. With scarcely a second glance at the shot-riddled vixen they hurried home to bed.

The 'earth' in the spinney had originally been the home of badgers, a home-proud species that even bring their bedding up in the sunshine to air. Now, with month-old cubs inside it, the sour scent of fox, combined with decomposing carrion, gave clear warning that only flies, fleas, and the most stupid woodland creatures dared ignore.

Restless with hunger and wide awake long before the bird's dawn chorus the cubs yelped and whimpered, waiting for a mother that would never come.

• Nature's law, the survival of the fittest, made the three healthiest cubs turn on the smallest, driving her from the den, up into the light.

None of the cubs had been more than a few yards from the main entrance to the 'earth', and only in the last few days had the vixen let them stretch out to sleep on sun-warmed moss. With her brothers' sharp teeth nipping at her haunches and raging hunger cramping her insides, the tiny vixen cub blinked up at the late spring sunshine, trying to scent the way her mother had gone.

At first the trail was easy, for the old vixen

had made a definite path. Dew and woodlouse did little to allay the thirst or hunger and by the time the cub had reached the orchard, her weak, wobbly legs refused to support her weight. She squatted on her haunches, yelping. A pair of crows, riding the thermals above the orchard, planed down to investigate the interesting sound.

Black shadows blotting out the warm sunlight bothered the panting cub, then she was suddenly surrounded by tearing talons, flapping wings and raucous beaks.

Passive, resigned to death, she was too exhausted to bite the small hands that rescued her from the crows' attack.

Suspicious of his bulging anorak, the boy's mother asked what sort of rubbish he had brought home this time.

'If that's a dirty old paintbrush hanging down from under your coat you can put it in the dustbin right away.'

Gentle as only the young can be, the boy's tears fell upon the cub he held out in his cupped hands...

'I couldn't leave it out there for the crows to kill, Mum. Mum, look at the white tip to the poor little thing's tail.'

The boy's mother was unenthusiastic. But eventually she was persuaded and 'Paintbrush' was established in a cardboard box den in the garden shed.

All summer long she was pampered and

petted, until a neighbour's kitten was found injured on the garden path.

An ultimatum was issued, 'that fox' must be destroyed.

An elder brother undertook to take Paintbrush to the vet. But once clear of the houses he headed for a forestry track. Deep into the woodland, the boy opened the car door and pushed the young vixen out. Through his tears he watched the white tip of her brush disappear into the bracken as he and his brother drove away.

Paintbrush, happy to be free of lead and collar, circled a plantation of birch and chestnut—then came back to the track to await the boy.

She waited for a while as he had taught her, then a vole rustled in the bracken. Paintbrush pounced, and missed.

Many hungry weeks elapsed before self-preservation had overcome all memories of feeding bowls and tinned dog food.

Winter came to the woodland. Soon after the nights began to shorten, Paintbrush heard a dog fox calling far away. Head held high and keening, she went towards his cry.

They met in the undergrowth of the old stone quarry and during the days that they ran together, they found shelter in a cave-like rock formation where the gnarled and knotted roots of a beech tree overhung the quarry edge.

A farmer saw them playing there, and Paintbrush, remembering the same scent of another human, hesitated. Then a badly-aimed shot confirmed her mate's frantic warning that their worst enemy was Man.

By the time the moon had grown full, waned and was full again, the young vixen had established a den among the undergrowth on the bank of the swift-flowing river in the game preserve section of the wood.

Pheasant and other game provided a full larder. And while the keepers tried to trap and out-fox her, her contact with humanity had left her with the insight to keep her safe.

Her cubs were never hungry, and by the time they had left her, the vixen with the white brush had attained notoriety among the hunting and shooting fraternity.

She had often heard hounds baying beyond the winter woods but they had never disturbed the game covert until, coming back to the den one morning, she found the entrances blocked. The scent of Man and dog was all around her. Paintbrush took to her heels and ran.

The huntsman's horn sounding 'away' warned the hunters that the vixen had broken cover and was running. She circled through a flock of sheep, then remembered that cars can make humans lose their scent.

Thundering hooves, and the pack in full cry, drove her towards her objective. As she streaked towards the motorway fence the first hounds were breath-hot near.

Dodging hurtling vehicles, she crossed both carriageways, and as she sank gasping into a ditch on the far side, pumping noises in her head blotted out the sound of mayhem on the motorway.

The vixen became an obsession with the hunt, and within days they were following her line again.

This time she led them out towards the quarry and when they were close behind her, she slipped down into the cave beneath the beech tree roots. Frantically reining in his horse the whipper-in watched his hounds race straight towards the quarry edge.

Word was given that anyone seeing the vixen with the white brush was welcome to take a shot at her. The keeper who did so, thought he had missed. His shots had penetrated her pelt and had begun to fester, making her body swollen.

When the hunt next found her scent the vixen was too exhausted to take flight and slipped into the river, hoping to throw them off her trail. The water soothed the throbbing soreness at first; then the cold made her lethargic and cramped.

Oblivious to the baying hounds swimming behind her, Paintbrush surrendered to the river and let it take her down.

Only the white tip of her brush was visible

when hounds and riders reached the river. Calling the hounds back to the bank, the huntsman sounded 'Gone away.'

OLD PRINCE

Showers and warm sunshine had encouraged a crop of weeds to grow among the sugar-beet that we were horse-hoeing. This made the rows of pale green seedlings difficult to follow, and caused some of Dad's extensive repertoire of forceful language to be brought into use.

Using the wheelmarks of the seed drill as a guide-line, I led Prince, a seventeen-hands Suffolk Punch, across the field as Dad tried to steer the horse-hoe between, instead of through, the almost undetectable rows of beet.

I did my best to follow his shouted instructions of 'To you. From you. Back-aways. Steady.' But they became increasingly desperate until his agonised 'Whoa there!' signalled that his patience could stand no more. We stopped.

'Blind and blast it. Six rows we've done, and all I've noticed is a dozen plants. Eight of those have been trampled under that cussed old horse's darned great hooves, and the rest I've cut up with the hoe.'

He checked that the flat-plated hoes were properly lined up, set three hand-spans and a thumb's length wide across the tool bar. Finding it correct, he concluded that there must be something radically wrong with the way I led the horse.

Some brief basic training on the art of horse-hoeing followed. Then we were off again. But not for long.

He was sure the hoe was not set too wide. I knew that I was blameless. So that only left the horse.

Prince was a moody, slow-moving, lumbering old gelding with an uncanny instinct for knowing when someone inexperienced was trying to harness him, or make him work.

A horse's working collar is extremely heavy. Getting it properly positioned requires some degree of co-operation between harnesser and horse. The principle is to place the collar over the horse's head, turned top to bottom, and then to give it a half turn once it has safely passed the ears. If a horse will help by holding its head down the job is as good as done.

When I tried to harness Prince he would stand with his head erect and his muzzle way up beyond my reach. If I attempted to thwart his craftiness by clambering on to the top of the corn bin and shoving his collar over his head from aloft, his head would go straight down.

Ignoring me completely, he nonchalantly munched his bedding straw with a supercilious look on his face.

If something upset him while he was working he would throw his hooves out wide and stumble along as clumsily as a man with size thirteen boots and two left feet.

Contrary as he was, he had one saving grace. When the spirit moved him he was the strongest horse on all the farms around.

Neighbouring farmers faced with waggons bogged down in the mud, or with loads that their own horses jibbed at pulling, would send for 'Harry's Old Prince'.

He always seemed to accept the challenge of this type of situation, taking the strains on his tug chains, expanding his barrel chest and making it all look too easy to be true.

Strong or not, it only needed two or three strides along the next row of the beet field before we realised that the cantankerous old horse had discovered a new way to annoy. He was moving like a car that has its back wheels out of line, planting his massive hind hooves down six inches to the side of where he had placed his fore.

'Cummup-aways Prince!' Dad hollered, but he might just as well have saved his breath.

Watching Prince's sideways progress, Dad called another halt and stood expounding improbable theories as to the horse's lineage. In his opinion, one of Prince's forbears had had a highly irregular association with a crab!

'The old devil's laughing at us. Two whole hours we've wasted standing around like "Go day, come day, God send Sunday!" 'Tis no use! You just hold those handles steady while I lead him to the end of the row, then we'll give it best.'

'I'll get Jim out here horse-hoeing tomorrow and if we fare no better I'll most likely plant the field again. Cummup, then, you old cuss!'

Led by Dad, Prince walked daintily, docile as a placid little cob. At the end of the row Dad said, 'Woa there, stand!' Instantly obedient, Prince stood with the full weight of his nearside fore hoof planted on Dad's right foot, and, despite all the shouting, seemed to be rooted to the spot.

Dad limped home to soak his rapidly swelling foot in a solution of hot water, comfrey leaves and Epsom salts.

As he sat there, immobile and cursing, he gave an appraisal of the moody old horse. Prince had an appetite to match his size. His unpredictable behaviour was a luxury we could ill afford.

Selling a horse was something Dad always loathed, but from a purely economic standpoint he decided that given a reasonable offer from a reputable buyer he would let the old horse go.

'Tiny' Robbins bought him, although it was more like an exchange and barter than a sale. The going price was £5 cash, plus an old self-binder—when it could be moved from behind some wagons and a dung spreader, at the back of Tiny's barn.

Three days later Tiny Robbins, six foot four, with a flame-coloured beard and temper, came striding into the yard.

'That damned old "hoss" is a wrong 'un, and you knew it. Lame as a one-legged duck! It is standing in my loose-box all of a tremble, with one leg off the ground. It's gone off its feed. You'd better come and fetch it, and I want my £5 back.'

Dad was anxious now and I accompanied him to Tiny's farm in case they had difficulty in bringing the poor animal home.

When Dad went into the loose-box Prince's drooping ears pricked up and the hoof that he had lifted went back on the floor. Among other things, Dad called him a crafty old devil. He suggested that I should take Prince out and walk him around outside.

'There's ten acres of winter wheat crying out to be ring-rolled,' Tiny raged. 'So what are we doing parading a "crocked" horse around the yard?'

'Crocked be blowed!' Dad said, or something like that.

He harnessed Prince and put him in the shafts of Tiny's ring-roll. Walking off with no trace of a limp, Prince went through the wheat field gate then up across the field. Dad handed over the reins to me and agreed with Tiny that I should stay and get the wheat rolled, since the horse was not as well behaved as Tiny had believed.

Within a week Tiny Robbins was back in the farmyard leading the dejected-looking horse.

'This ruddy object is not a horse, it's a menace. He has broken two sets of shafts and a gate-post, now he is acting lame.'

Prince rolled and ran as skittish as a colt the moment he was turned out to graze. The next time that I tried to harness him he actually held his head down as I put his collar on.

'I don't reckon we'll try to sell the cunning old devil again,' said Dad, when we were back indoors.

'It wouldn't do for him to be too sure, though, or he'll start his crab-walking and footcrushing antics again.'

SIGNS OF SPRING

From an enveloping carpet of wide-eyed daisies and lush spring grasses the mate of a nesting skylark ascends in a singing spiral to predict fine weather for the day.

All Heaven may be echoing to a chorale of early-morning birdsong but this will pass unnoticed by those head-scarf-turbanned, pinafored housewives of the village, who, like rooks repairing last year's nests, have risen with the lark and blackbird in their enthusiasm to begin refurbishing their homes.

Sunny weather and the blacksmith's wife have decreed that this is the moment to begin spring-cleaning. Apart from the feckless few who are content to let this year's crop of dirt obliterate last year's pride, the fear of gossiping tongues forbids that any of the rest should lag behind.

Few chimneys emit the hazy white drifts of smoke that every other morning of the year signify dry kindling wood flaring beneath a kettle set to boil for the first brewed cup of tea.

Instead, the grates are cold and cleared of ashes. Furniture in the rooms with fireplaces is systematically moved. Curtains, cloths and coverings await baptism by wash-tub.

Mirrors, family photos, and gilt-framed pictures removed for cleaning, uncover unfaded patches of wallpaper that like unmoving shadows stay to claim the right to an allotted space on the overcrowded walls.

Rugs and mats—rolled up, dragged out to the yard and beaten—hang limply, waiting to be revived with the soapsud water that remains in the copper when the orgy of laundering is done.

None of this process can start until the chimneys have been cleaned out thoroughly. On this bright sunny morning the womenfolk keep an eye on the Forge House chimney to watch for the sight of a sweep's brush emerging, or, better still, the telltale puffs of smoke which signify that, with soot cleared out to Slippy Springer's satisfaction, the fire is drawing nicely even with damp wood.

This morning however, there is obviously something wrong with the time-honoured arrangements. Almost seven a.m., by chimney sweeping standards late on in the morning, and the blacksmith's wife stands impatient in her doorway. Slippy, our local chimney sweep, is nowhere in sight.

His wife, too happy-go-lucky to join in the annual rites of spring is taking Slippy's lurcher bitch and puppies for a morning constitutional across the village green.

'Slippy is very late in coming to sweep the chimney this morning.' The blacksmith's wife registers disapproval of having her spring-cleaning timetable turned topsy-turvy for the day.

'So he will be!' Slippy's wife is almost nonchalant as she gives the reason for her spouse's absence. Once again Slippy's catapulting prowess has been unable to withstand the temptation of a high-flying cock pheasant in the close season and, in the words of his long-suffering wife, our Slippy has been 'took down for fourteen days'.

A fortnight is too long to delay the start of spring-cleaning when, for most women whose husbands do land work, it is the last chance to get their houses in order before they begin their own seasonal work on the farms.

The landlady of the Hare and Hounds, having heard about Slippy's sentence, has already contacted a sweep from the town.

He arrives at opening time, breathless and bad-tempered, charging what, by country standards, seems an exorbitant price for scattering the half-shovelful of soot he's got out of the chimney over himself, the kitchen, and everything he touches. He retires to the tap-room, to emerge at closing time too befuddled to know which way he can get home.

A whole day wasted, fires are lit in rooms still stripped for cleaning. Husbands, loathing the upheaval, make idle talk of probably taking a brush and a 'binder' to that old chimney, come Saturday afternoon, hoping against hope that a benign justice will see its way clear to giving Slippy remission on his sentence before Saturday comes.

Meanwhile there is nowhere that a man can sit down in comfort, and even those stay-at-home men who only cross the Hare and Hounds threshold on the Mutual Brotherhood Club subscription nights slip out to find some sort of peace in the taproom, unless they are prevailed upon to help heave Gran's feather mattress out into the backyard to beat it, thus relieving some of the frustrations of a soot-inconvenienced wife.

It is left to Violet, a hefty lady of inexhaustible energy and uncertain temper, to provide the solution. Violet will borrow Slippy Springer's chimney-sweeping rods and brushes, charging the same price as he would have done, but giving Slippy's wife a far larger percentage of the proceeds than that lady would have received had her husband not been 'detained'.

There will be no nonsense about starting at Forge House first, or dodging from house to house in order of preference. Violet will start at one end of the village and end up at her own home. She says she will start early in the morning, and this is exactly what she means.

Six a.m., four houses visited already. Tackling her task with an enthusiasm sadly missing in Slippy, Violet dislodges the soot of years. Children are dispatched outside to watch for the brush emerging. Minutes later Violet is on her way again.

The chimney-sweeping set includes drain clearing equipment, which Slippy wheels from house to house in a truck. Scorning such weakling notions, Violet heaves the lot up on to her shoulder and, whistling, strides on.

At Forge House the blacksmith's wife, impatient of waiting, helps drape the sackcloth cover across the fireplace of the cavernous chimney and watches Violet send brush and one cane rod after another up into space.

No children here to shout that the brush is out of the chimney. Instead, they must rely on the farm men waiting in the smithy yard while Bert the blacksmith shoes their horses or mends their hoes. But men enduring the spring-time upheaval of snatched cold dinners and discomforts are apt to be less than helpful.

Tom Grommett, who this morning has discovered too late that his wife had treated the lavatory seat with some quick-drying varnish that wasn't, watches as the brush sways like a long-stalked, frost-blackened sunflower over the rooftop, then curves gracefully down to touch the road. It rests beside a grating made to send storm water pond-ward. Tom lifts the grating and directs the brush to a watery grave.

In Forge House, Violet realises that all the rods are used up and wonders if the brush has found its way into the space beneath the roof. She strides outside to study the roof span, and sees the cane rods arching from roof to drain.

Ignoring the smirking males who watch her, she stamps back into the house and starts to haul the rods back down. As the brush re-enters the chimney, something obstructs its progress. Violet heaves and a brushless length of rods comes clattering down.

An upheld candle, illuminating the darkness, shows iron rungs that sweeping boys once climbed. Violet marches forth outside. Tom Grommett has temporarily disappeared.

The only men around are the blacksmith and Treacle Budd, who has just dropped by to leave a billhook for Bert to mend.

Bewildered, Treacle is engulfed in a sooty embrace as Violet lifts him bodily in a boa-constricting hug and carries him into the house.

Prodding him with cane rods, she encourages him up into the chimney to bring the brush back down. His ordeal over, Treacle staggers to the yard wall, his eyes still starting from his grimy face.

Watching Violet's departure, Bert marvels at the widow's energy and strength. Violet, of course, once went away to marry, returning just in time to bury her husband here. Now Treacle expresses the opinion that there is probably an empty coffin buried in the churchyard.

''Tis my belief old Violet crushed him up and ate him, I tell you Bert, she had me mortal feared! I reckon her stove in half my ribs when she grabbed me tight.'

Treacle nurses his bruises, the women indulge in a plethora of soap, paint, wallpaper and sticky polish made from turpentine, resin and shellac.

Slippy, in prison, has avoided this year's bout of spring-cleaning and there are men in the village who say that he is no fool.

A SUMMER STORM

The periphery of the pond had become a dried out, sun-kilned saucer, the surface crazed with cracks by the drought.

Like the last foul scrapings of fermenting broth, the stagnant water stank of decayed leaves and rusty iron, unfit for farm stock to drink.

With piped water still an amenity we only dreamed of, an alternative supply for the thirsty cattle meant hauling up water from the well in the kitchen garden.

Letting down the heavy wooden bucket to the rusty limits of the winding chain and winding it up again time after time, until the tank of the water cart was filled, was a long slow process indeed.

Time was at a premium that morning. 'Shup' Woolley had arrived to start shearing up in Ten Acre sheep pens, with only a wall-eyed collie and Old Jack to help him, on a day when Dad had left early to go into town for the annual Soft Fruit Sale.

Our cherry crop was among the lots to be auctioned. We had high hopes that bidding would be keen. Being short of cash and man-power it had seemed safest to sell the cherries outright rather than risk engaging casual labour and marketing them ourselves.

Several interested wholesalers from the larger fruit markets had walked beneath the laden trees in our orchard, and all had acknowledged the prospect of an abundant crop.

The birds, too, showed great interest in the ripening Early Ambers and Dark Rivers. They were enjoying a thirst-quenching, fruit pecking field day undisturbed.

When I finished hauling water I went into the house to fetch Dad's old twelve-bore gun and some blank cartridges, to scare them away.

Mum was in the dairy, flushed and flustered, churning cream that she was sure would turn sour before it ever became butter. Around her feet was a gaggle of vociferous goslings that had ambled in through the open door to escape the heat.

Breathless—'Can't stop churning. Pesky things are asking for water in their splashtub—

The cheese pasties I've put in the oven for Shup Woolley and Old Jack will be burned to cinders—And take them that stone bottle of cider you'll find on the pantry floor.' Pink-faced, perspiring, perpetual motion in a pinny, Mum.

I left Mum to her churning, rescued the shearer's 'elevenses', and shushed the goslings outside.

The cattle over in Mockbeggar Field started bellowing for water as soon as they heard the rumble of the iron-wheeled water cart clanking out of the yard and down across the meadows.

The airborne escort of swarming flies, circling effortlessly around the horse's head, transferred their attention to the shearers when I stopped to give them the cider and food.

Old Jack, who by rumour slept in all his daytime clothing with the exception of his 'wellies', seemed impervious to their irritation, but Shup swished at them with his cap and asked me to bring him a branch of elder back from the tree in Mockbeggar Field hedge.

'Nothing like elder sap to keep them hot-footed varmints from worrying, if you don't use too much and get dozy-yudded.' Jack said.

To Shup, elder was 'witchwood'. It could bring nightmares, lethargy and blinding headaches if one stayed too long near its scent.

'Look yonder,' said Shup. 'There'll be a storm afore many hours.'

A small cloud, white as the new-shorn sheep,

hung on a horizon that shimmered in the heat. By the time the drinking troughs were filled up in Mockbeggar, that one little cloud had become a distant range of celestial, high-peaked mountains.

As I took Shup's elder branch back to the sheep pens, he suggested that I brought the cart over to take the newly-shorn fleece down to the barn.

We loaded the wool clip, watching the fast-moving, ominous cloud banks, grey on black, white on grey, tinged with ochre in the searing sun. A sudden-sprung wind set circles of dust swirling; the branches of the Scotch Pine by the sheep pens swayed overhead.

'We'll ride back to the barn with you,' said Shup, 'If we stay here, we'll get a wet shirt.'

The rain reached the yard as we did. Spots, big as florins, hit the hot stones. With the grumbling thunder coming nearer, I hurried into the house, knowing that Mum would be hiding in the dark 'glory-hole' cupboard under the staircase, terrified of the storm.

From its depths I received instructions to cover all the mirrors and open all the doors and windows to 'let the lightning out'.

Purple, blue, and crackling, the lightning discharged its fury amid thunder that smothered the sound of my mother's sobs.

Just when the storm seemed to be passing came a noise like a persistent, furious drumming.

'Oh, God!' Mum rushed to the staircase window, crying in anguish. 'Hailstones! Look! The cherry orchard is white.'

The torrential rain rushing down the yard had blocked the gully, flooding the kitchen inches deep in water and mud. As we mopped up the mess we saw a fruit wholesaler's lorry stop in the lane by the orchard. The driver surveyed our ruined crop.

When Dad came home he told us that our cherries had been valued at £500 before the storm came. After the storm, when the sale started, he could not get one bid. Five hundred pounds to us was a small fortune. He sat with his head in his hands.

Shup Woolley came to the back door with the empty cider jar.

'Harry, I reckon we're middling lucky. The pine tree up in Ten Acres has been split by lightning and the ground all round it scorched to a cinder, yet with all your ewes penned up under it, you haven't lost a sheep.'

'You have to be lucky sometimes,' said my father. 'Come on in, Shup, and we'll crack another bottle of cider to celebrate our luck.'

WHOLEMEAL AND PLAIN

Tom Barker was convinced that his two rat-catching tortoiseshell cats tried to forewarn him, probably saving his life, on the day his mill blew down.

With both mill and livelihood gone, Tom was leaving the village. He went down to the Hare and Hounds in the hope that the landlord or one of the customers knew of a home for the two cats.

'Strange creatures, cats,' Tom soliloquised. 'All morning they'd scudded round scratching, clawing and "raising up a wind", so I knew that we were in for a bad blow. Sure enough, by dinner time, the old mill were swaying and creaking as she always did in a stiff sou'westerly wind, but everything looked safe and secure to me.

'Them cats knew different. Fair drove me dizzy with their worrying and hollering round my legs, or chasing down the steps into the yard.

'Back they'd come, all of a fidget, with their eyes aglow as if they had seen Old Nick himself. I began to wonder what was up, so I thought I would slip across to the house and get them a drop of milk to see if that 'ud stop their pestering.

'Dang me, I had only just got to the kitchen door when I heard the old mill groan like a soul in pain, and saw her tumble down like a house made from cards.'

Tom looked as if he had relived that moment again and again since that terrible day.

'I reckon that there's something mighty uncanny about animals as can tell what weather is coming. My old father used to say that they could smell danger, and see ghosts.'

'Very likely,' The landlord's tone of voice indicated that the subject was now closed. There are many deep-rooted folk legends and country superstitions concerning the supernatural activities of cats, and like most old-fashioned countrymen, the landlord thought it unwise to meddle with matters that could not be easily explained.

But the cats were still 'unadopted' and it was not just gratitude or affection for them that made Tom reluctant to condemn them to run wild.

That, by Tom's beliefs, would mean that wherever he went their spirits would come searching for him. To kill them would 'down his luck'.

Knowing that there was always a collection of domestic pets, tamed wild animals and birds at our place, someone suggested that he should bring them up to us.

He stood in the kitchen, with the cats mewing in a closed basket on the floor. Mum, hovering indecisively, was not sure that she could cope with two more mouths to fill with food.

'Take 'em, Missus. You know they're lucky, and I promise that from today, you'll not be worried by the sight or sound of rats or mice.'

It sounded a pretty extravagant claim, but Mum had to admit that in all the sacks of flour that she had bought from the mill there had never been the slightest sign of mouse droppings. Cat's hairs yes, but they were a different matter. Like the threads and strands of sackcloth that often got ground in with the flour, they detracted nothing from the flavour of the bread.

Where, she asked, were we supposed to keep them while they were getting used to their new home? I suggested the old attics for a start.

Our house was centuries old. The walls were thick, and it was full of crannies and corners where field mice, seeking winter quarters, made their homes. When the old house settled down to creaking slumber, the silence of the candle-lit night-time would often be disturbed by rustlings and scampering noises above the bedroom ceilings as mice and sparrows took up residence in the old attics overhead. As they scuttled round, it sometimes sounded as if they were holding marbles tournaments.

Mum agreed they could stay, if I would take on the responsibility of looking after their welfare until they settled in.

The rest of the house had always had a noticeable atmosphere of tranquility and happiness, as if generations of contentment and laughter had soaked into the walls. This the attics lacked.

In the eighteenth and nineteenth centuries when farm servants were engaged on a yearly basis with food and shelter included in their pay, they took their meals in the farmhouse back kitchen and slept in the cramped, sloping attics under the apex of the roof.

Two sets of ladder-like steps on the back landing originally led to sleeping quarters for the unmarried males on one side and the maids' attic on the other. Both were white-washed, but drab and spooky, with tiny dormer windows that let in precious little air or light.

All our sweeping, singing, or opening of windows, never seemed to dispel the impression of sadness, as if there were lingering echoes of the privations that the old attics must have seen.

Far more substantial than echoes of the former inhabitants was the evidence that the attics were now harbouring mice, or even rats. The miller's cats were needed up there.

'You realise that we can look forward to regular swarms of kittens?' Dad was less than delighted when he came home from the fields, and we broke the news.

It was too late to alter the situation. The two cats were up in the attics with their paws already buttered, and looking as if they were quite prepared to stay.

For the next few nights, sleep was scarce and frequently interrupted. Overhead the two cats waged a vermin-destroying war.

Within a week they had become as much a part of the family as the pet lambs, the three-legged rabbit, a young magpie that would hypnotise itself by staring at its reflection in the hub caps of parked cars, and a crippled, talking, jackdaw with only two words in its vocabulary, one of which was rude.

Within a month the cats were answering to their new found names of 'Wholemeal' and 'Plain', tolerating my affection, but following Dad around the farm as though they had been trained to walk to heel.

It didn't pass unnoticed. Emmy's Mum, who in the summer came to help pick the fruit, was only one among those who said that the miller's cats were unnatural beasts. She would

130

never allow them in her home, in case they gave it the 'haunts'.

Picking apples in the orchard Mum happened to say that 'Wholemeal' was washing behind its ears to make it rain. When it did, Emmy's Mum scuttled home convinced that she had witnessed witchcraft at its worst.

Nevertheless, when Emmy's eyelids were incessantly plagued with styes, her mother brought the grubby-faced child to ask Mum to help cure the complaint. Mum suggested clean water, soap, and a freshly-boiled face flannel, with egg-cup baths of diluted boracic lotion for a start.

That was not what Emmy's mother had in mind. Her recipe for her daughter's cure was to brush the child's afflicted eyelids with the tip of a lucky tortoiseshell cat.

We waited for signs of either cat having kittens, but neither did. 'Wholemeal' was at least twelve years old when she died, but 'Plain' was with us until we learned that our land was to become part of a huge new housing scheme.

LIKE A LOT OF SHEEP

When March meant my acting midwife to a flock of lambing ewes, the hours that I spent among the thatched hurdle-gate shelters in Ten Acre Field were lonely, tedious, and long.

By the time lengthening days had forced the tight-fisted hawthorn buds to give the hedges a sprinkling of green, I knew each sheep by name. No two sheep look alike, and among my flock were some that bore an uncanny resemblance to some of my relatives, in features and personality as well.

One ewe, thin faced and quick to stamp her hoof, seemed to shun the hurly-burly of the feeding troughs, but, for all her unassuming manner, managed to get more than the rest. Aunt Flo to the life.

With her socially inferior sisters giving way, another ewe, obviously the 'lady' of the flock, would stalk imperiously towards the troughs, with never a wisp of her thick smooth fleece out of place. She had the same haughty bearing as my Aunt Bertha, whose husband owned a drapery shop.

This ewe would lamb in the warmest shelter and need more attention than most. Her lamb always demanded mama's full attention, bleating if she should graze too far away. Aunt Bertha's daughter reacted in exactly the same way.

Aunt Bet was varicose of veins and extra outsize. It was she who brought a family wedding reception to an uproarious finale by going up the garden path to the 'outback'. She had returned, screeching like a barn owl, with her fleecy-lined bloomers around her feet.

A stray hen, sheltering in the darkest corner of our 'one-holer', had shown resentment at her intrusion by taking hefty pecks at her behind.

We laughed *with* Aunt Bet, never *at* her. With every overweight pound of her quivering with merriment, she would have been the first to realise that one of my flock had a serenity of features and disposition to match her own.

Like her human namesake, this sheep got into the most improbable situations. I once found her nonchalantly chewing the cud with a feeding bucket jammed down on her head.

Now I marvel that a ewe would be placid enough to let me approach and pull it off. But at the time there seemed nothing incongruous in reporting to Dad that I had found 'Aunt Bet' on her back with all four legs in the air.

Just through the hedge, their celibacy enforced by a sheep-wire fence, were the two rams. They too had traits recognisable in our own kin. One was hard-headed, fat, and inordinately preoccupied with eating, which in a nut-shell summed up Aunt Bertha's husband, Uncle Fred.

The other would chat amiably with his erstwhile wives through the wire, or wander to the far fence to cast a roving eye over the young ewe tegs in Banky Meadow. Uncle Bill had the same inclinations too.

If every family fold has its straying sheep, Uncle Bill was ours. He thought it pointless to worry about earning money that he couldn't take with him when he went, and if his flirtatiousness went too far Aunt Bet had an unfailing method for settling scores by waiting until he slept and sitting the whole of her sixteen stone on his chest.

Like our methods of stock rearing and farming, the bizarre and colourful characters of earlier generations seem to have no counterpart today. The mould that turned out my sort of Uncles and Aunts seems to have been lost, broken, or thrown away.

Take the year that Uncle Fred realised his

ambition to become chairman of his district council, and a magistrate to boot. This coincided with the tercentenary of a charter giving the place the right to hold a weekly market in the main street.

Neither event had the slightest impact on the inhabitants. But Uncle Fred, with an eye to business, started his Charter Celebration Scheme.

There would be a pageant, a torchlight procession, fireworks, and a fancy dress dance to round off the day. All this would give a fillip to the pre-Easter doldrums in Uncle's drapery shop.

Each neighbouring village was invited to send a beauty queen as candidate for the Miss Charter contest. Riding on their village float, each would take part in the parade.

The floats were to portray some local historical event, but the only thing that seemed remotely historical near us was that 'Treacle' Davey's great-great-great-uncle had been hanged for rustling sheep. We settled thankfully for that.

There was no swim-suit parading to choose our village beauty queen. Uncle Fred was one of the judges. My statistics were as vital as a beanpole so I didn't even enter.

Spring lambing was no time to dream of parading around the town on a jazzed-up cart. Plump Ethel was the obvious choice, since she had a salmon-pink bridesmaid's dress left over from last year.

To Uncle Fred there was one small cloud on his Charter Celebration sky. He confessed this in the sanctity of the family circle at Sunday night tea.

'Remember that night at the city fair? Can't we find Bill a job to make sure he be not led into temptation again?' Somehow, Uncle Bill was persuaded to lead the horse that pulled our float.

Ethel in her satin, topped by a thick-knit woolly cardigan to keep out the cold, sat on her curtain-covered throne, sharing the float with two penned sheep, four gawking yokels, one hangman and a life-like, straw-stuffed, red-oxide bloodstained body swinging from a gibbet above her head.

In company with some of the other villagers I got a lift back home in the fruit farm lorry, so it was the next morning before I knew that anything was wrong. Uncle Bill was in trouble, serious enough for Uncle Fred to convene a family gathering at our place.

'Me, the council chairman, and a magistrate too,' he stormed, 'I don't think there would have been such a fuss if that policeman hadn't been so shook up.'

Uncle Bill had only been trying to get the matter into perspective. On the face of it, it must have been un-nerving to the constable to hear a horse approaching in the darkness, and to find it pulling a mobile gibbet, with the

136

driver curled up in the back between two sheep and a bloodstained corpse.

Uncle Bill, fearful of being summoned for being drunk in charge of a horse, equally afraid of being sat on by Aunt Bet, and longing to catch up on the sleep he had lost in the police station cell, slipped stealthily out into the lambing pens in Ten Acre Field.

'I tried to tell 'em that the old horse knew the way home a darn sight better than I did. He weren't drunk and nor were I.'

As he watched the sheep flocking around me as I went towards the troughs, he observed:

'Joan, gal, does it ever strike you that some of the folk we know acts like a lot of your old sheep?'

WOOD SMOKE ON THE SEASHORE

The horizons of my life were peopled by a profusion of relatives. Some regarded our old farmhouse as a haven, knowing that their welcome would be generous and warm. Others had only perfunctory contact with us, but all would be remembered on Sunday evenings when Mum undid the clasps of a leather-bound family album.

She would sit at a cumbersome, round mahogany table in the front room, turning the pages, and turning back the clock. As I looked and listened, I learned who was who, and why.

There were aunts in hats that only needed clotted cream on them to transform them into fruit salads; uncles photographed in Army uniform or in their Sunday-go-to-meeting best;

a ferocious-looking grandfather; overclothed and over-inflated babies, wedding groups, studio portraits, and fading sepia prints.

The man in the picture on the last page was my father's uncle who lived on an isolated part of the coast some fifty miles distant.

Sitting in an uncomfortably-carved, throne-like chair, he looked awkward and embarrassed. A peaked cap rested on his crossed knees and a medal hung from the thick, dark, sea-going jersey that he wore.

Standing beside him, straight-backed and as shapely as a clothes-post, was a poker-faced woman, severely dressed in a plain white blouse and a long serge skirt.

'Is that his wife?' I would ask, knowing full well that it was not. Mum would then relate the story of a shipwreck and rescue, culminating in Great Uncle Thomas being presented with a medal by the King. After the ceremony he had been photographed with his sister.

I liked the way Great Uncle's eyes crinkled up at the corners, but was not at all sure about Great Aunt.

'Aunt Dolly is a terrible upright sort of woman,' Mum admitted. 'She would mend your manners if you ever went there to stay.'

The threat subsided for communications between the cottage on the cliffs and the farmhouse became more infrequent especially since Aunt Dolly regarded it to be a wicked waste to spend money on writing paper and stamps.

Imagine our bewilderment and confusion when, after two years of silence, a telegram arrived from old Aunt Dolly, cryptically worded:

'Indisposed. Send female help at once.'

Uprooting Mum was out of the question, so I became the unwilling 'female help'. I had little experience of nursing human beings, but could by that time dose a horse, deliver a calf, or cope with a cow with colic, so was deemed capable of dealing with any eventuality that might arise.

While Mum packed my bulging hold-all which Dad lashed to my ancient bike, I took a private peep at that last photograph in our old album, just to convince myself that Aunt Dolly did not appear to be as grim as I recalled. She did.

As the branch line train transported me and my bike towards our destination, I prayed that time would have mellowed her, or that I would be given the courage to turn tail and ride back home.

There was a twelve-mile ride between the railway station and the cottage on the cliffs and although I had never been there before, Dad's oft-repeated description of the area made me recognise features and landmarks along the way.

The sheer beauty of the last part of the journey, where the twisting lane seemed as if it must drop down into the sparkling sea beneath, was unexpected, and as I free-wheeled down it, with the wind blowing my long hair out in all directions, I saw the picture-book cottage, applied protesting brakes and came to an unladylike stop.

As I picked myself out of a hedge of fuchsia I heard a frail but imperious voice remark, 'Trust Harry to send some scatterbrained hoyden with unkempt hair, displaying her legs'.

This was my Great Aunt Dolly. At eighty-plus, she had broken her right arm and damaged her left leg. She had fallen hauling a load of seaweed up the cliff to provide manure.

She informed me that Uncle Thomas would probably be idling his time away down on the beach, but since I was supposed to be there to help I had best get started.

I still remember Aunt Dolly's broom cupboard as a brush salesman's nightmare, with dozens of cleaning brushes hung around. Blacklead brushes for cleaning the steel and iron stove, soft brushes, hard brushes, cornice brushes to sweep imaginary dust from picture rails and the curtain rings that held thick, dark curtains shutting out the light. Birch-twig hearth brushes and wickerwork bats for beating hearth rugs, I used them all that first afternoon.

By evening I was tired and famished, but had to be content with two caraway wafers and a drink of goat's milk—after I had milked the goat.

Still sitting bolt upright, Aunt dozed into a cat-nap, and since Uncle Thomas had not put in an appearance I walked down the cliff path to explore.

The smell of wood smoke drifted up from the seashore and as I walked towards it I found Uncle Thomas sitting by a driftwood fire in a small cove among the rocks.

'Thought you would find your way down here sooner or later, Harry's young 'un. Sit you down and talk.'

He had the eyes of a mischievous old pixie and as he explained that his sister was 'a good intentioned soul beneath the burrs and prickles' he added that 'When it comes to grub she was parsimoniously inclined. What she eats wouldn't fatten a parrot. Still, if you can keep a still tongue we'll find ways to get round that.'

From behind the rocks he brought out an iron pan and some cobs of bread tied up in a cloth. There on the beach we had a picnic supper of fresh-caught mackerel and bread.

Home seemed a long way off that night at the cottage, but at first light the next morning I was too busy to think of anything but work. The first job was to turn the feather beds and air them and Aunt Dolly, watching over me like a keeper, asked why I had not 'doked' the beds. I had not the slightest inkling of what she meant.

Disgusted, she came back, hobbling along with a thick stick as support.

'Did your mother never teach you, girl? Now, beat up all the feathers so there are no valleys or hummocks in the bed. Don't you know that the devil could take possession of you if he can get into the shape you left in the mattress when you got up?' Nothing would appease the old lady until this was done.

Bread-making was another task Aunt was sure I could not deal with, and while I had helped my mother time and time again I was not too sure of the old beehive oven at the cottage, but decided to have a go. Uncle had escaped to the rocks when I began and, having set the dough to rise, I started chopping wood to light the oven fire.

Suddenly Uncle came running up the cliff at a pace that would have given a heart attack to most men of his age.

'Don't light up the bread oven, girl', he hollered. As he rescued some bottles that he had hidden in its depths he whispered: 'I used to hide many a cask and bottle in here when the customs men came calling when I was younger. Now I only hides it from old Doll.'

Uncle Tom and I got on famously and even Aunt Dolly admitted that if I stayed long enough she would probably be able to teach me some sense.

But her injuries were healing fast and one

evening she caught Tom and me having a clandestine supper on the beach.

'Gourmandising and giving way to gluttony and greed', she called it, although it was only a pullet's egg apiece and an extra loaf I had baked for Great Uncle Thomas.

Next morning, much thinner than when I left it, I went back home.

WHEELS OF PROGRESS

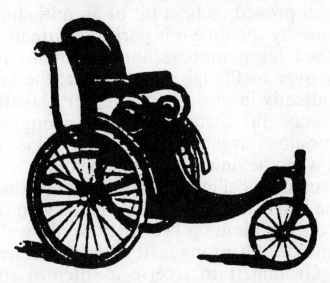

Services that people in urban areas took for granted were extremely slow in reaching outlying districts such as ours.

We knew that, given time, the wheels of progress must inevitably turn in our direction, although they always tended to get bogged down and broken-axled on their way.

So infrequent were the changes in our way of living that the importance of the most mundane innovations tended to become magnified out of all proportion.

The siting of the first telephone box in the parish caused as much excitement as if it had descended from the sky.

It was arranged that as soon as the Post Office engineers had connected it, the chairman of the parish council would declare it officially open, and make the first formal call to the mayor of the nearby market town.

It all proved to be a bit of an anti-climax, because by the time our parish chairman had changed his gumboots and driven his milk lorry over to Plough Lane corner, the kiosk was already in use. The innkeeper's layabout son was in there holding a long and acrimonious argument with his bookie, and even when he finished, Tom Grommett's wife was standing belligerently by the kiosk door.

She had arrived first, and anyone who tried to stop her phoning her sister would get the rough side of her tongue. It took some time for Mrs Grommett to receive a stitch-by-stitch detail of her sister's major abdominal operation.

Our local dignitary was getting impatient and hammered on the kiosk door, but having invested sixpence in phoning her sister Mrs Grommett was determined to use every second she had bought. Six pennies in those days bought a lot of telephone time.

When the chairman was finally free to declare the kiosk open his only audience were the ducks and geese that had waddled over from the pond on the off-chance of being fed.

Two passengers alighting from the market day bus displayed no interest at all. Even the formality of his official phone call had to be cut short when he discovered that he had only one penny to be swallowed by Button A.

The mayor he was phoning was an auctioneer by profession, so cutting the social niceties to a minimum our local chairman took the opportunity to discover the latest selling price for barren cows and in-calf heifers, before the line went dead.

Although power cables had begun to etch black lines above our lanes and hedgerows, none of the houses in the village had been connected to the mains power supply. So the fact that it was illuminated by electricity made the new phone box unique.

That one small, harsh light seemed to shine out like a beacon in the darkness at the far end of the unlit village. It attracted moths and maybugs and on Friday and Saturday evenings the lads and lasses of the village used to congregate within the circle of its light.

Girls, whose parents believed any artificial aids to beauty were snares of the devil and forbade their daughters to use make-up, took advantage of the illuminated mirror above the telephone directory shelf to try out the lipstick and powder they would never dare to apply in the candle-lit bedrooms of their homes.

The old saddler in Plough Cottage found that the phone box saved him money. On dark evenings, when the weather was not too bad, he would take his stool, a newspaper, and his glasses, and settle down in the phone box for a quiet read.

147

There were those who felt sure there must be some law forbidding such practice, but he would always willingly vacate it if someone wanted to make a call.

As he said, it was a darn sight less draughty to sit in than Plough Cottage and the light bulb certainly made reading easier than did a smoky lamp.

'There's folk what are jealous because they don't live handy enough to take advantage of new inventions, as I can', he would tell his critics. And in their hearts they knew him to be right.

Not everyone was sure that the arrival of electricity in the village was a good thing. To be able to make light and heat without flames or fire smacked of dark practices.

Deep down superstition made the older generations extremely wary of the invisible power that lay in cold wires obeying switches, yet could kill a man in much the same way as lightning in a storm.

Fear of electricity caused old Grandfather Chapple, the dairyman, to put a spoke in the wheel of progress, making for months of litigation and legal argument, because he was convinced that if the authorities put power lines across his pastures the dairy herd grazing beneath them were in constant danger of curdling their milk.

Progress was slow in other directions. If The Season's Collection meant high fashion and dress shows to town dwellers, in our language it meant the quarterly visit of the rubbish-collecting cart.

My father held a contract to provide a driver, horse and wagon to accompany two council employees to each dwelling in the parish, four times every year.

One might well believe that with thirteen weeks between each visit the village would be inundated with refuse, but in fact very little was collected on the rounds.

Almost everything we used seemed to be disposable, serving as fuel for the open fires, food for backyard fowls, or compost for the garden. Even tins served as rut fillers where iron-banded cart wheels cut deep into unmade tracks.

Iron bedsteads were traditional materials for cottage garden fence mending. Old discarded mattresses were dug into the soil to improve its tilth. Rags served the same purpose, unless they were sold to the old rag-and-bone man who travelled around the area with a creaking cart and a skinny pony.

It was considered perfectly honourable to inspect other people's rubbish heaps just before collection day in case they were discarding any article for which one could perhaps find a use.

Children, too, found this to be a profitable pastime, collecting empty bottles and returning them to the back door of the Hare and Hounds, at a penny a time.

The vicarage rubbish was sacrosanct, but when the parson's sister hid the evidence of her 'little failing' by disposing of the empties down the burrows of the rabbit warren up on Lockley Bank, we all knew there would be no profit there.

Nothing was considered too large or too small to be carried away by the collectors, but errors were sometimes made. Their round went as far as Tyler's End Cottage, where a cantankerous old man lived with a daughter whom he brow-beat into believing that the shock of her engagement had made him unable to walk.

For years she pushed him around in a wicker bathchair, until the collectors found it by the cottage rubbish heap and carried it away. The old man walked two miles to retrieve it, and pushed it, buckle-wheeled, the two miles back.

A month later he walked his daughter up the aisle.

One day a steam lorry delivered twelve gross of toilet rolls and a huge drum of disinfectant to our farm. Dad had no knowledge where it came from but the council sanitary inspector told him to distribute it all around the village when the next collection took place.

Toilet rolls were a complete innovation, making excellent tracing paper and, with health hints printed all over them, much too interesting to waste.

150

Not everyone was happy to receive the free samples and some even more unhappy with the results. The old saddler, meeting Dad in the village, said so, but Dad replied it was a sign of advancing progress to try to kill off germs.

'Progress, be blowed!' said the saddler. 'I put some of that stuff in my old bucket and emptied it on the garden. If that's progress ... it's killed off all my beans.'

HARVEST HOME

Lamp-lit in the dark of a misty autumn morning, one stands in the icy flag-stoned passage trying to conjure warmth from a coat as chilled as the farmhouse door from which it hung.

Thick rubber boots make damp and clammy contact with stockinged feet still blanket-warm from a reluctantly-left bed. But until the day when cattle can stroll into the kitchen and actually say they are hungry, Dad's creed is that no one will sit down at our breakfast table until the stock have all been watered and fed.

Picking up the paraffin lamp, you draw back door bolts that some eighteenth century blacksmith fashioned strong enough to withstand a siege.

With lantern bobbing, you cross the cobbled yard toward the stables, since they are nearest and warmest. There Turpin, Tom and Ginger rise from their oat straw bedding in greeting, snuffling round pockets as you fill their manger racks with hay.

Inquisitive, curly-coated bullocks, fluorescent-eyed in the shadows of the cattle yard shelter, come across toward the gate, each making its own patch of mist in the finger-chilling air.

Tommy, the hen's Rhode Island romeo, annoyed at being caught off guard and wakened by the earlier-than-usual feeding, crows his disapproval and flaps around his chuntering complaining wives.

A bellowing, bucket-reared baby calf, hurdle-gate penned and separated from its mother, cries plaintively to be fed and as if in answer the lowing cow calls back. Dad, sitting on a three-legged stool and rhythmically filling a pail with milk, tells them both to stop their fidgeting; there's more than enough for us all.

Indoors again and the kitchen fire, that had been damp twigs smouldering under a kettle when last we saw it, has grown into a warming welcoming blaze.

Eggs in the pan, strong tea sweet enough to almost support a spoon vertically, and a round-table conference decides how best to tackle the extra tasks that the last Saturday in October always brings. Each year we are sure they will never get finished, but each time the day ends crowned with success.

Dad, wanting to get the ploughing forward while the weather is holding, say he'll put in a couple of early hours in the furrows of Ten Acres, in case the pheasant shoot heads in this direction, for it wouldn't be the first time that 'His Lordship's' party of guns had peppered the horses.

Meanwhile there is a flock of ewes over in Stony Meadow to be checked and counted and since it is almost daylight the coats and boots go on. It is time for work again.

There is the feel of ground-frost on the air, with mist in the valleys, and against the backcloth of a pearl grey sky, a skein of wild geese, flying south, call to each other as they turn in the direction of the estuary. The quiet air whispers with the music of their wings.

A shiny black beetle in the tall couch-grass by the field gate marches doggedly through the mist-drenched near-impenetrable green grass jungle. One wonders what vital and essential beetle mission forces him to tackle such a formidable, and to human eyes, completely useless task.

Wood pigeons fly up, calling a warning from the distant poplars skirting Barn Field, and an inborn knowledge tells you that someone or something hostile to them is moving under cover of the furze and tall bracken along the rough ground by Church Wood.

It will probably be old Slippy Springer, for yesterday and the day before there was a tell-tale trail of corn strewn down among the brown and dying bracken, enticing 'His Lordship's' pheasants to feed at their will.

Today, or perhaps tomorrow, when their numbers have increased substantially, their diet will be much more exciting, and the raisins that Slippy's old lady said she was buying because she fancied a bit of Christmas pudding will be whisky soaked and scattered amongst the corn.

Drunk and incapable of flying, the pheasants will go quietly and without gunfire to an intoxicated doom.

The flock of ewes and Bill the ram are all present and correct and just over the fence in Plough Lane pasture, mushrooms shine up white and plentiful.

Today, because it is the last Saturday in October, it is permissible to hop over the fence and pick them, then hurry back to the farmhouse to tell Mum that in this day of marathon baking there is something extra to cook. At least there is time to lend a hand.

Baskets of sweet apples, washed, cored and dipped in melted butter and brown sugar, are baked by the trayful and as they leave the oven Conference pears by the dozen take their place. Tonight the apples will be eaten, soft and sweet flavoured, encased inside a butter-toffee shroud.

155

It is mid-day before we know it. Someone remembers there is still a wagon load of folding chairs and trestles waiting to be taken from the chapel to the village hall.

Our village hall, no more than a hut, is a scene of disorganised chaos, with fruit, flowers, crockery, borrowed sheets and crepe paper, all piled up among the stacked trestles and chairs.

Smoke rises from countless kitchen chimneys, heating this special Saturday's bath water, boiling puddings, or mountains of mashed 'spud'.

Doris, at the village store, reports a run on shampoos, brilliantines, hair curlers, and collar studs. While Shortfoot Price the travelling draper makes a special journey with an urgently-needed and outrageously-priced dress.

Stock, fed earlier than usual this morning, will be fed again and bedded down even earlier tonight.

By tea-time there is hardly a house in the village where flatirons are not putting a final crease in best blue-suit trousers, or pressing the seams of a hastily finished frock. Seven thirty. All the hours of preparation have been worth it. The Hut is transformed into a land of plenty. Chairs scrape on the uneven floorboards, tables creak, and our customary Harvest Supper begins.

Vicar and Chapel Preacher sit together, and set an example by their friendly chatting, but each tries to outdo the other in eloquence as we stand through two long-winded variations of saying Grace.

Tea pots, jugs and even cups have coloured wool tied on their handles so that the owners can be traced.

Ladies with hair just released from rat-trap wavers and steel curlers have covered their best dresses with frilled satin pinafores. Squeezing between tables they carry unbelievably huge, piled-up trays of food.

Generous as ever, 'His Lordship' has sent over hares and several brace of pheasant, roasted in The Hall kitchen, and neighbours remark to one another:

'Pheasant? Fancy! There's a rare treat!'

Old folk like Granny Gammon and Old Dubber, who find that chewing pheasant comes hard to toothless gums, are advised to try Mr Springer's feathered rabbit pie. They know and we know what is in it, and if the head keeper up on the top table is too dim to realise, it's because his glass has been emptied as often as his plate.

Ladies, too dignified to drink ale from the barrel, are pressed to try each other's home-made wine. When the tables are dismantled and the centre of the floor cleared for dancing, they giggle, perspiring freely, and watch the proceedings in a rose-hued glow.

Old songs are sung and best boots squeak as they dance to an out-of-tune piano and a violin. The floor joists of the wooden hall creak and groan.

Five minutes to midnight, three hours past our usual bedtime, we sing the National Anthem and laughing, face the long walk home.

THE EARTH SPIRIT

The oldtime countrymen called it Lammas-tide, those early August days when Beauty of Bath apples ripened on the tree and the first golden crops were fit to harvest in the fields.

I used to watch those old men scything around the edges of the cornfields, preparing for the self-binding mower to make its initial circuit without beating down the standing crops.

Old men, working waistcoated despite the heat, mopped their brows on huge red-spotted handkerchiefs that dangled from their belts and stopped for the occasional drink from screw-topped bottles of cold black tea.

Invariably the last dregs of each thirst-quenching drink would be tipped on the ground. Had anyone suggested to old Jimmy Yellows that by spitting out his last mouthful of tea he was subscribing to old pagan beliefs and placating the Spirits of Earth and Harvest, his response would have been to dismiss all book-learning individuals as being 'a bit wet under the thatch'.

Now, when I think of Jimmy Yellows, memory etches every detail of a Lammas-tide day and a harvest field where pre-Christian custom and the twentieth century met.

If the Earth Spirit walked in our oat field that morning she had cornflower blue eyes, wore a cobweb bejewelled veil of scarlet poppies in her flaxen hair, and had a thistledown fringe of ox-eyed daisies around the hem of her dress.

Oats make a good-tempered crop to harvest, soft-strawed, silky to the touch, not prickly spiked like spiteful barley, or as hard-headed and heavy to carry as wheat.

Impatient to get to work on the cutting, I brought the tractor and self-binder to the gate, to find old Jimmy Yellows leaning on his scythe.

There was still a fair distance for him to mow before I could get started, so I went 'taking out' and 'bond-making' behind him, gathering the cut corn into sheaves and binding them with bonds of twisted stalks, using exactly the same technique as Ruth or Naomi did in biblical times. I must have shown impatience at the old man's plodding slowness.

'I don't know why you're in such a tearing hurry so long as most of it's down and stooked by nightfall.'

I knew Dad had reckoned on cutting all the oats and starting on the barley crop up on Mockbeggar by nightfall, but Jimmy dismissed this suggestion with disgust.

'It ain't right and proper not to leave the last bit of corn standing overnight', he said, deeply serious. I asked him why. He couldn't really say, except that the old 'uns never did it.

Now I know that earlier, more superstitious generations believed it to be expedient to leave the last few swathes standing at the end of the day, in case the Spirit of Harvest, lurking in the fields, had been forced to retreat by the advancing reapers. To catch sight of it would bring disaster. Better to be safe and let it make its escape after dark.

Once I could get around the field on the tractor, with Dad working the controls of an ancient self-binder behind me, Jimmy began collecting the bound sheaves of corn we were cutting, grouping them together in long straight rows. The grain would have been harvested just as well if the stooks had been placed haphazardly, but it offended any countryman worthy of the title to see untidily stooked fields.

All was going well, with the tractor chugging around and around the field. Our old self-

161

binder, noisily protesting, rattled at being taken out on its bumpy annual outing.

The tractor I was driving was a noisy lease-lend American giant, hired from the County Agricultural Committee because our own Florrie Fordson had gone into decline and collapsed in a heap of scrap iron and rust. Florrie and the old self-binder would have understood each other's weaknesses; the American job, throttled right down, was too energetic for the binder. With the field half finished, its main drive wheel fell to bits.

Passing Jimmy on my way to ask the blacksmith if he could work miracles, the old man reminded me he had warned against foolishly talking about finishing the field before night.

No immediate miracles were forthcoming from the blacksmith, but talking to him in the smithy was the County Agricultural Committee contractor, responsible for the hiring of machinery on loan.

At a time when every grain of corn grown counted, he could appreciate the quandary we were in. The solution he proposed made me jittery. A revolutionary implement called a combine harvester would be standing idle all that afternoon while its driver went for treatment for his aching teeth. The driver's mate would be available to advise, direct and take care of all the other machinery if I could just sit at the controls and steer it round the

162

field.

Showing great confidence in his daughter, my father agreed to hire it. I couldn't eat my dinner—I felt sick and nervous.

Jimmy Yellows stood awestruck as I climbed up on to the scarlet and yellow monster. It was steered by two levers. Being left-handed, that foxed me from the start.

Yawing, slightly zig-zag but mostly forward, we were off. Overconfident, I moved the levers less warily. The machine veered sharply in Jimmy's direction. Escape for Jimmy meant a high leap over a quickthorn hedge.

We stopped engines, Jimmy emerged, complaining that he imagined the word Dodge on the front of the machine to be the maker's name and not a warning, then stamped off to the far side of the field.

A fault, not mine, developed in the combine's machinery. As we admitted defeat and went homewards, Jimmy said that perhaps in future I would know better than to talk too loudly about completing the cutting of a cornfield before night. Strangely enough, the combine worked perfectly the next day.

THE FORGE YARD WALL

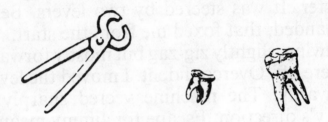

Today Church Wood was discarding the last remnants of autumn and we walked amid a shower of falling leaves. Only the rustle of our footsteps disturbed the quietness and no birds sang.

There was the same sense of stillness in the lane, as if the countryside was enjoying a brief tranquility before the winter storms.

Even the village street seemed deserted, except for Will and old Mr Applethorn, who were sitting on what used to be the forge yard wall.

For centuries the old men of the village must have chosen the same spot to sit and gossip in the sun, for there the wall is lower by several inches. The stones have a rich patina, smoothed and polished by contact with innumerable seats.

Now, Bert's forge has been demolished, and the yard where once the white convolvulus twined around old harrows and broken ploughs has become a private patch of short-shaved sterile lawn.

But the customs of centuries die hard and, private property or not, the old men still sit sheltered on the forge yard wall to watch the world go by.

As we passed, I commented on the quietness of the afternoon.

'Quiet,' muttered Will, glancing along the deserted street, 'you would think everyone else had been carried off by plague.

'Saturday afternoon and no one about because they're all watching sports programmes on TV.'

Old Harry Applethorn, frail and fragile as the autumn leaves, nodded his agreement and paused from puffing at a stubby pipe that provided a form of central heating for his nose.

'Love my days, Will. If I'd told my old workmates that there'd come a time when folks were content to spend their free time watching pictures moving in a little box, they'd have carted me off in a padded van for sure.

'If they found time to sit around on a Saturday afternoon, it's like as not they'd be just where we'm sitting now.'

'I've seen the time when there's been a row of

us old farm boys lined up like "spadgers" along this wall, all waiting for "Shup" Woolley to get round his sheep and come down here to cut our hair. It wasn't deserted then.'

The blacksmith's forge was traditionally the pulse of the village throughout the working week. Although it was closed for shoeing on Saturday afternoons, it provided a meeting point for the men of the village to exchange gossip and cabbage plants, a place where they could sharpen blunt billhooks and hoes, a venue for Shup Woolley's various skills.

If the weather turned bad he set up shop in Bert's 'pantus', the space where horses were usually shod.

In fine weather his barber's chair was a saddle-stone in the forge yard.

His customer sat with one of Bert's muleskin aprons tied around his neck. While Shup got busy with the same shears that he used to clip his sheep, bystanders and waiting customers gave their comments on his styles.

Not that it worried Shup. His philosophy was that there was only a fortnight's difference between a bad haircut and a good one.

He used the same technique for his tonsorial efforts as he did for shearing sheep, starting with a deep sweep through the middle at the front and progressing in even ridges toward the back.

His customers wore crew cuts long before crew cuts became a fashion. Shup called it

166

'shearing 'em up close', to keep the hair out of their eyes during the six weeks of lambing time, when he would be too busy to get down to the forge.

It was strictly 'First come. First served', and if a customer had brought his horse to be 'clipped out' it took its turn with the rest. Shup used the same clippers, regardless of his client being man or beast.

His versatility was great if his tools were few. He carried a pair of special pliers in his pocket. In spring these were used for gelding male lambs and docking their tails, but they were available for other uses throughout the year.

Anyone with a dental problem and a nerve of iron could sit on the wall and wait for Shup. His strong wrists could whip out a troublesome tooth in as little time as it took to dock a lamb's tail.

Advance warning that Shup was 'drawing teeth' ensured that there would be 'standing room only' along the wall.

Reluctant little lads who bawled at the prospect of one of Shup's haircuts were reduced to instant, snivelling submission with the threat that 'Mr Woolley had his pliers in his pocket' and sat close-lipped, cross-legged and flinching as Shup's sheep shears flashed around their ears.

Since there were usually more men around the forge yard on Saturday afternoons than the entire congregation at Sunday church, the parson often dropped by to try to even up the balance and give notice of forthcoming festivals and mission magic lantern shows in the parish hall.

These were well attended by women and children, but the menfolk were a different matter.

On one occasion, when the parson explained that the lantern lecture was about nomadic tribes that wandered over Africa grazing their cattle and sheep, one or two of the men decided that they would like to see these 'foreign' breeds of stock.

Shup Woolley was among them, sitting beside his prim, no-nonsense wife. He sat enthralled, slide after slide, commenting loudly on the bony cattle and sheep that, in his estimation, had been too friendly with a goat.

The parson, manfully reading on despite the interruptions, told his listeners that the women of the tribes tended the flocks in these uncivilised lands.

He stamped his foot and as the next slide showed a scantily-clad nubile female, Shup announced gleefully that he for one would willingly undertake to 'Learn that sheep-gal summat different from 'er heathen ways.'

Mrs Woolley, whose proud boast to the local ladies was that Shup had never seen her in less than her combinations, used her umbrella in the same way as her husband would use his crook, hooking the handle around his windpipe and hauling him off outside the hall.

The following Saturday the parson came to the forge yard to remonstrate with 'the sheep that strayed'.

'After all, Shup, you are one of my flock. For in my way I am a shepherd, too.'

'That's as maybe,' Shup said, solemn faced. 'But I don't reckon you'm kept so powerful busy come your lambing time, that you're out of your own bed, night after night, like me.'

Despite his brushes with the parson, Shup had a sincere, uncomplicated belief in the hereafter, with all his hopes for eternity centred on his old smock.

Made of coarse linen, it was virtually tick and water proof by reason of the lanoline from the fleeces of his sheep. It had been his father's before him, and it was his pride and joy.

'When I gets to knocking on them big gates, The Gaffer's Son 'ull say "What you want up here then, boy?" and I'll tell Him that I am a shepherd too. He'll see my smock and know I'm speaking the truth. "Come on in, then, and give an eye to they old ewes," He'll say.'

As Shup saw it there was one problem. He couldn't go to his Maker in a dirty smock and prayed he would choose a good drying day to die.

He did, but as Will and old Harry Applethorn remembered, there was a 'rare old panic' getting Shup's smock washed, ironed and aired in time to put him to his rest.

''Tis all quiet and different now,' said old Harry, tottering stiff-limbed off the wall and staring at the lawn-covered old forge yard.

'You coming along with me, then Will? By the time we toddles back and switches on, those wrestling chaps 'ull be up to their capers, and us don't want to miss that.'

MOONLIGHT ON THE MARSH

'I don't really belong round here, you know,' Tom paused to pulverise a morsel of birthday cake with his toothless gums.

His middle-aged daughter poured tea into a thick white cup and passed it across to the old man.

'Don't you start your old yarns, Father. You know you were born and bred not twenty mile away.'

'Twenty mile?' Tom took a sip and continued.

'It might as well have been two hundred. Nowadays you wouldn't credit folks would stand to live like it.'

'So you've told us.' Half apologetic for her apparently curt manner, Tom's daughter whispered: 'The old chap does go on so.'

To hear about the different way of life that only the old can remember is to me like hearing a haunting melody played far away. Once the tune is finished there is no way to recall it; the music is lost for ever as each note dies away.

As long as I can remember, Tom has been acknowledged as one of the best sheep men in the district, tending the huge flocks out on the marshes until rheumatism and old age forced him to give up.

Now he is comfortably cared for by his daughter in the village, but his mind wanders back to the open marshes and the old cottage under the leeward side of the pollard elms, where marsh and ploughland meet.

At this, his eighty-fifth birthday tea, he had every right to his memories. I encouraged him to go on.

'How old was I when I came here? Fourteen or thereabouts, and I thought I was a full-blown workman then.

'A farmhand's life was only tolerable if you had a fair-minded master. If you were stood off every time bad weather kept the horses in the stables, life was just mud, work, hunger and hell. One word out of place and it was "Out of your cottage before next Saturday week".

'My father went in mortal fear of offending the landowner who employed him. If the gaffer said he wanted a field cleared at a shilling a load, then all the family from mother to the youngest toddler in petticoats got out there picking up stones.

'Stones grow, you know. You would start at one end of the field and work through to the other, and by the time you'd finished, there'd be another crop of stones on top of the soil again.

'Anyway, I was out in those wet old fields helping my mother, and the little 'uns crying with cold, when the gaffer and the farm bailiff rode over and asked if I could read and write and count to a hundred at school. I took my father's old cap off, ducked my head as we had been taught to do, and told them I could.

'"Right then," said the gaffer. "You'll start as boy to the shepherd when he comes down to the yard on Friday. Get your things together and go back up with him to Moorbanks to help him with his sheep."

'No question of whether I wanted to go, or if my father would permit it. The landowner had spoken, and that was that.

'So off I went up to Moorbanks where the gaffer ran enormous flocks on five hundred acres of rough grazing on the hills. It was a seven-days-a-week job looking after that lot. The shepherd and his boy were the only ones on the estate excused from Sunday services, because we could never be far from the sheep.

'Rough living? Most of the old farmhouse up at Moorbanks was empty and falling down with damp. There was just the shepherd and

173

me up there, and he was a rum one. Smarmy, quiet spoken, and mighty religious in front of the people who employed us, but a terrible heathen in his habits when we were alone. I got so scared I went and slept in the old dairy where we stored the wool clip. Then he told the gaffer I'd been in there deliberately ruining several fleeces.

'I tried to explain, but the gaffer said he wouldn't listen to a parcel of old nonsense about a man who was trying to be a father to me. Besides, good shepherds were hard to find.

'"Fatherly, my foot," I thought, not daring to say what I was thinking. As I stood there taking a tanning with a sheep-crook I said to myself, "Thomas, it is time you wasn't here!"

'Where could I run to, and how would I earn a living? Next day, up in the hills, it seemed as if the Good Lord answered that. The air was so clear I could see blue water and the coastline in the distance.

'The shepherd asked me if I could see white patches on the marshes yonder, and said that each of the white blobs was a sheep. I knew then where I would head for, and when the shepherd went down to the main farm the following Friday, I was off over the hills toward the coast.

'I ran as if Old Nick was dogging my footsteps, and next day when I went through villages I had never heard of I was still scared I would be hauled back.

'The village bobby stopped me by Foxley Cross Lanes early on Sunday morning, and made me empty all my belongings on the grass. I saw that the direction finger on the signpost said Marshside, so I told him I was a shepherd going there for a job.

'Try as I might, I couldn't find the way to the farm on the edge of the marshes, so it was evening before I eventually trudged up the lane. A pony and trap carrying folk Sunday-dressed for chapel, came up behind me.

'The gentleman driving said he would not talk about work on a Sunday, but the lady told me to go to the back door and wait.

'She fed me a great plate of cold mutton, and before I realised it I was telling her all about the place I had left. The gentleman came in soon after and said they were sheep-dipping the following morning and I could have a week's work to help out.

'That week lasted sixty-nine years, and I reckon I knew every square inch of the marshes. I'd give anything to be out there on a moonlit night in winter. The wild geese will be flying over and coming down on the marsh to graze.'

Tom was suddenly lost in contemplation. Out through the window, a big round moon was well up in the sky long before the sun had gone to bed. We had a full moon, a car, and old Tom with a birthday wish that was easily granted.

Excited as a child on Christmas morning, he sat in the back muffled up in rugs. Past the signpost where a policeman once stopped him, down to where a row of pollard elms marks the length of the long straight lane. When trees and lane both ended we drove out across a gated track.

With the risen moon and faded sunset making a mockery of twilight, we followed the track across the grey-green marshes to a shepherd's hut within twenty yards of the sea wall.

Out on the saltings the sea lavender whispered, and a making tide in the estuary sent water chuckling through the runnels scored deep in the grey mud. Mallard made much ado as they planed onto the mud flats and an arrow-swift flight of teal rushed by.

Back in the car, Tom was getting impatient. 'Wind down the windows. Keep still and listen.'

We heard the wind in the dead marsh grass and the mallard quacking, then a sound like a vixen baying far away. As it came nearer, we would hear the geese calling to each other, their powerful wings beating a vibrant rhythm as they rode the air. The skein of geese flew low in V formation, outlined against the full moon. It seemed that the air quivered with a million flying wings, then a flight of peewits, sensing our presence, gave an alarm call and the night was still.

The moon made the shadows of the elm trees rush up the lane toward us as we drove homeward. Our minds were still bewitched with the lonely sound of wild geese flying. The man who had shown us the magic of this haunting music was curled up in a cocoon of contentment, fast asleep.

THE PRAIRIE PROWLERS

In hedgerows that in more seasonable years would be bending in submission to the steel-tipped lash of January storms, pairing birds survey new meeting sites and sing full-throated songs of spring.

In meadows where the winter-dormant grass is usually brown with cold, or rimed in unthawed frost, this year's cattle find good grazing and farmers who last autumn forecast a lean and hungry winter for their livestock, give thanks for each succeeding frost-free, grass-growing day.

I remember another January when we counted our blessings along with our sleek, plump cattle.

Daffodils bloomed with the snowdrops

along the garden path that year and the prunus tree by the churchyard gate shed blossom like snowflakes, falling on wallflowers flowering months too soon.

Taking stock of the situation, Dad decided that the mild weather had saved enough of the reserves of feeding stuff on the farm to invest in a few more 'store' cattle. These he would fatten in readiness for the springtime sales.

Indulging in incomprehensible mathematics with a piece of chalk on the corn-bin lid, he estimated that even if the weather broke and we were snowed in at Easter, we could still manage to maintain half-a-dozen young bullocks, providing he could acquire them at a reasonable price.

'Reasonable' to my father meant something between half-price and next to nothing.

Banking on the unlikely possibility that the market prices would be hovering near rock bottom, Dad decided that come next market day he would catch a bus to town.

I willingly accepted his invitation to accompany him, although it meant getting all the milking, feeding and watering of stock finished before seven o'clock breakfast.

There was just time to try to tame my recalcitrant hair into an 'up-swept' hairpin-anchored style. If it looked as if my cranium was covered in small, over-cooked bread rolls it was much more fashionable than the one long plait that usually served to keep it tidy, hanging like a sick pig's tail straight down my back.

I polished my high-heeled 'town' shoes that for smartness, if not comfort, were worth every penny of the guinea they cost. Wearing a new coat that had taken months of rabbit-catching and selling to buy, I caught the market-day bus to town with my father, feeling smart as new paint.

'Who's the young filly then, Harry?' The auctioneer's clerk left his rostrum in the market to edge close to me, acne-faced and leery.

I rewarded his interest with a disarming smile and my high heel near the lace holes of his patent leather boot.

Every 'skin and grief' sag-boned old bovine that the market porters ushered into the selling ring was hailed as 'a first-class young beast', or, 'We've got a beautiful little heifer here'.

Even so, the prices that the bidders were paying went higher than Dad's budget would allow.

Before he slipped away to see what other stock was on offer in the cattle pens, Dad gave me a tentative finger for the pen of steers to be sold next.

To follow and understand the jargon of a quick-talking auctioneer is to understand a strange language with no sentences, no pauses, a monotonously droned monologue.

As soon as the bidding started I realised that the only bidder opposing me was the owner of the half-dozen, rough-coated, wild-eyed, unpolled steers that were careering round the ring.

A friend of my father's nudged me.

'Steady gal. Let him buy those prairie prowlers back.'

'The bidding is against you,' the auctioneer looked hard in my direction. I shook my head and looked the other way.

My last bid was still below the price limit Dad had set me, nevertheless I could see that for all their roughness, the steers had good lines and well-proportioned bones.

Reassured by my father that I had made the right decision, we stayed on, missing out on mid-day meals, although breakfast felt long gone.

Most of the pens were empty. Some cattle were loaded into carts and lorries, others driven away by the hard-swearing, hardworking drovers who would undertake to deliver cattle and sheep unaided and think nothing of taking them twenty miles to their new homes.

By the market clock I knew that we must either leave to catch the village bus, or walk the five miles home.

'It's a pleasant afternoon for walking,' said my father. My 'town' shoes were uncomfortable and I could see little reason for staying on.

By now the bidders had decreased

considerably and as the market porter prodded a thin, subdued little Hereford bullock into the sale ring, he said,

'There ye are sirs, I've saved the best till last.'

Salvaging one of the hairpins from my slipping 'Bread Roll' hair-do, I thought aloud that the man must be joking, and found that the auctioneer had mistakenly imagined that I was signalling a bid.

No one else even bothered.

'Clever girl,' said my father, 'That little fella's ours at a very reasonable price.'

All hope of catching the bus home had vanished, although it wouldn't have been the first time that a calf had ridden home 'child's fare' on the Flying Dutchman's bus.

It looked so forlorn I hardly knew whether to drive it or carry it, but Dad had a fair length of binder twine in his pocket, and like a puppy on a lead, it trotted beside me as we made our way back through the almost empty pens. One pen was still full and in it were the six 'prairie prowlers'. Waiting beside it was the man who had tried to raise my bid earlier in the day.

'A deal, Harry?' he called, and after much head-shaking, walking away and arguing, Dad agreed to take them off his hands. By the time the deal was settled and paid for, the market was deserted apart from men with shovels and sweeping brooms.

So there we were, Dad, myself, a timid Hereford that seemed to derive consolation from licking my best new coat, and six rangy steers, raring for freedom.

All transport was fully booked, the drovers had all departed, but his 'exceptionally reasonable' purchases brought out the optimistic streak in Dad.

'Not to worry,' he said nonchalantly, 'We'll walk them home gently ourselves.'

He wasn't wearing high-heeled shoes that made his feet ache. I was and felt hungry as well.

Even that raised no problems, by his reckoning. Were there not piles of running shoes on a trestle table outside the 'cheapjack' stores on the corner of Market Street? I could call in for a pasty at the pie shop as we sauntered down to the far end of town.

'Saunter' is not the word to describe our progress. Those bystanders who did not retreat behind the safety of closed shop doors, helped us shoo our little herd in the general direction we aimed for.

Any idea of doing business at the cheapjack shoe store seemed best forgotten when one of the steers took a dislike to the goods on offer and knocked the trestle table down.

The church bells pealed as we headed down the High Street. A photographer, posing wedding guests on the grass outside the church gate, found his grouping rearranged by a perspiring farmer, a galloping girl and seven stampeding steers. We did not stay long.

183

As we passed the pie shop at a steady canter, I reflected that it would seem somewhat unethical to ask for a steak pie when the yearling Hereford trotting along beside me was convinced that he was closely related to my coat.

Apart from a detour around the brewery loading bay in Quay Street we made good progress until shops gave way to suburban gardens and open gates. A house-holder of a close-curtained residence, opening his front door the following morning, must have been perplexed to find a cow-pat on his doorstep along with the morning milk.

There was no moon and no traffic to speak of after we left the lamp-lit outskirts of town. With grass verges to graze, the pace slackened to a steady walk, until one steer found a gap in the iron bedstead fencing of Dubber Wall's vegetable plot.

The others joined him in an onslaught on two rows of winter cabbage, and it took much shouting and chasing to drive them off.

In recompense for the damage caused, Dad offered Dubber a load of manure delivered free, but Dubber was fiercely independent.

'Don't know that it calls for a load of horse dung. I reckon I'd better turn that over in my mind.'

At last we reached the farm road, with Dad content that we had spent a profitable day. My feet throbbed, my hair felt like last year's birds' nests and by the yard gate the blacksmith's son stood waiting, home on unexpected leave.

A meal, a wash, the high-heeled, mud-plastered shoes discarded, and within the hour we were walking beneath the drifting petals of the prunus tree by the churchyard gate.

The falling blossoms looked like confetti in the moonlight, and in the mildness of that January evening we made plans for when it would be spring.

PUNCH

The gypsies, pitching camp to begin fruit picking, released the bantams that always travelled in the pot-box behind the wagon's back axle, then tethered their ponies to graze the lush long roadside grass.

Among the grazing skewbalds, piebalds, and broken-kneed old 'roarers' was a spirited young white gelding. It seemed to Stan to be the most magnificent creature on God's earth.

My brother Stan was then at the youthful gangling stage where his trouser legs were always parting company with his ankles. Although he was almost as tall as my father, he still spent several moments before the damp-speckled kitchen mirror every morning, surveying every aspect of his face in the hope that enough whiskers had sprouted overnight to justify a shave.

While he was brave enough to face up to the largest lout in the district, his deepening voice was liable to turn traitorously treble in moments of excitement, and he was easily moved to tears.

Stan never understood why the white horse should have had this disconcerting effect on him, but when he saw the arrogant gelding standing with both hind hooves hobbled by massive clogs of wood, and with its head still held high in defiance, the tears streamed down his face.

He ran home to remind Dad of a promise given that he, like his two elder brothers, would soon have a working horse of his own.

'Come and look at it Dad. It's way past seventeen hands high and I'll bet it's strong enough to shift a two-horse wagon. The gypsies wouldn't overcharge you, seeing that you give them work each summer. Come on, Dad, let's go and see if old Mannie Lee will do a deal.'

It was true that Dad could use an extra horse suitable for Stan to work with because at that time, when farming was heading for the financial doldrums, Dad was trying to keep on speaking terms with the bank manager and provide his men with full employment by contracting to haul timber from the forest to the sawmills, and by doing other contract work.

He said he would look at the horse later and sound out Mannie Lee as to its price. Stan went back down the lane to the gypsy horses.

To pass the time while waiting for Dad's arrival, he pulled a bag of sticky toffees from his pocket and tried to salvage the edible, gooey pieces from the torn paper and pocket fluff.

The white horse turned its head, its ears pricked forward in inquiry.

'Do you fancy some toffee then, old fella?' Stan approached, his hands extended. The horse snuffled, then laid its ears flat back and showed its teeth, its nostrils flaring in disgust.

'Either take it or let *me* eat it, then.' Stan patted the arched neck, reassuringly running his hand through a long, white, wavy mane.

He stood for a long time, confiding all his hopes and plans for their future, if only the gypsies would sell for a reasonable price. The horse stood, quiescent in the summer heat, letting Stan keep the tormenting flies from its head, brushing them off its body with a fetlock-long fly-swat of a tail.

Strands of the swishing white tail caught up in the great lumps of wood that were hobbling the horse's hind legs, Stan went to free them from the rough bark.

He did not notice Mannie Lee approaching with my father. All he heard was the gypsy quietly entreating him to get well back from the horse.

Stan stopped to untangle the last few strands, then, running his hand along the horse's withers, asked what was wrong.

'You must have been born lucky, chavi.' Mannie looked quite pale beneath his tan.

'That "grai" (horse) has the devil inside him and would flatten you into the earth, given half a chance.'

Dad said it didn't seem a very good prospect to buy it.

'I'd be the last Rom in the world to turn away a deal Gov, but that grey is a killer. He's broken a didakai's leg, smashed up two sets of shafts, and stove in the front panels of a "vardo". We're trying to take the steam out of him, and by fall of leaf we'll get him over to sell at Stow Fair. By then we'll have broken his spirit, and he'll be as placid as your old one-eyed mare.'

Dad started to walk away, but Stan, appalled at the prospect of the white horse being 'broken', was driven to the point of desperation trying to prove the gypsy wrong.

He went to the horse's off hind hoof and undid the leather thongs that held the restricting 'clog'. Mannie took the 'dickla' neckerchief from his throat to wipe his perspiring face.

'Strike me, chavi! Don't let his back legs free. It took four of us to get them hobbles on.

'Dordi! Guv, on my mother's grave, I'd not

189

let that killer go to a "cushti" bloke like you until we've broken him in, or killed him trying. He'd eat your young shaver soon as look at him. No Guv, that old grai is not for your boy. He's a devil and no mistake.'

Dad shrugged his shoulders and walked away, thinking Stan was close behind him, but Stan had moved round to take the near side hobbles off.

'He's not a killer, Dad, don't you see?' Tears took hold of Stan again, and he sobbed into the horse's neck.

Dad said that a horse that would stand that sort of performance couldn't be all bad. He would save Mannie a season of hard work and the worry of 'breaking' the white horse in and buy it at a reasonable price.

After the ritual argument, walking away, then hand-clapping to seal the bargain, Stan untied the rope halter from the heavy length of tethering chain and led the horse away. He remembered something.

'His name?' Mannie laughed. 'He's a clown, all ready to make a fool of you if you don't watch him. You had better call him "Punch".'

Punch had the end stall in the stable; with all the time and attention Stan lavished on him, Stan might as well have lived there too.

No one else was allowed to feed or groom him, anyone who tried found themselves dodging flashing hind hooves or sharp, nipping teeth.

My older brothers and Harry Applethorn began complaining that the best brasses and bridle ornaments 'fell off' their horses' sets of harness to reappear, burnished and jingling, on Punch.

Stan traded two ferrets and a second-hand pushbike to buy an old Spanish pack-saddle. Each Saturday afternoon I helped him to clean the three hundred separate pieces of brass.

The boy with the showy, pure white horse and smart turnout became part of the city's market day panorama. We proudly displayed Punch at horse shows, but he was only docile and willing to work with Stan.

Stan the boy, became Stan the man. Farming became another name for poverty, and the days of horse-drawn timber tugs and contract work carts were coming to an end. Stan, like my other brothers, was forced to find work elsewhere.

The stables which had once housed ten horses, now held three—Turpin, a stolid bay; Jim, my chestnut horse, and Punch.

Although he was temperamental and barely tolerated us, there was no question of selling Punch. He was Stan's horse, and therefore one of us.

I took over his grooming, which made Jim moody, and at times they seemed less like hefty cart horses than spoilt brats.

Throughout the hard-up 'rabbit for dinner' days, Punch and Jim, Dad and I worked as a

191

team, then a moronic casual labourer mistreated Jim, causing him to bolt and fall with an overloaded cart. Jim never worked again.

Punch and Turpin were incompatible as a ploughing team, so we bought a new horse, Tom. Punch was now my cart horse and at night we would hear him knuckering to Jim in the stable, like two old men discussing work. When Jim met a horrifying end trapped in coils of Army barbed wire, Punch kept vigil by the field gate, mourning with almost human grief.

Turpin, Tom and a tractor were now our work force, Punch seldom worked at all.

Dad's farming career was ending, and we were faced with a sale. The other two horses posed no problem, but what of our old Punch?

Stan took time off to help prepare for the farm sale. Stiff-legged and seldom out of his loose box, Punch greeted him with nuzzling joy.

Two mornings before the sale, Stan went to the stable, with Dad following.

'I can't bear to think of selling Punch to a horse slaughterer,' Dad said, glumly.

'No need, Dad,' Stan answered, his voice quavering as it did when he first saw his beautiful white horse. 'The old boy looks as if he has just laid down and gone to sleep.'

THE DEFENDERS

I was just eighteen, and in the spring-cleaned sunshine of that golden summer I cycled along the blossom-scented lanes.

Happily pedalling down and around the top bend of Lockley Hill, I almost collided with our portly village policeman, proceeding on his way up.

For a moment there seemed no way that I could avoid him. He stood lost in thought, leaning on his County Constabulary issue bike, right in the middle of the narrow road.

Taking a swathe of cow parsley from the nearside bank along with me, I skimmed by him, and as I free-wheeled on down, heard him shout 'Oi' and 'Stop!'

My front brakes and I would willingly have

obliged him, but the back brakes were past making instant decisions with the weight of two crates of broody chickens and Mrs Grommett's Buff Orpington cockerel in a basket lashed on to the carrier at the back.

There seemed little point in wasting pedal power down through Lockley Bottoms by stopping, when it was free-wheeling all the way to the Grommett's smallholding down at Chapel End.

The back door was wide open and in the empty kitchen a whistling kettle boiled in shrill impatience on the stove.

There was no sign of Widow Grommett.

Anxious to deliver the fowls and to get back up Lockley Hill to tell the constable that I had not tried to flatten him, I knocked on the door and called out to attract some attention.

I knew that for the last few days Tom Grommett, who ran the smallholding for his mother, had been engaged in work of national importance. At a time when invasion was a very real threat, Tom was dismantling all the signposts in the district and stacking them in our old barn.

There, remnants of the Dunkirk-rescued army, who had found temporary quarters in our brick-built corn store and granary, had acquired them for stoking up their field-kitchen coppers under the horse chestnut trees in the stable yard.

The old lady had to be somewhere on the

smallholding, because Tom was certainly not at home. Less than an hour earlier I had watched Tom solving the problem of hiding the unmovable rock-hewn milestone at Plough Lane corner.

In the name of King and country he had commandeered a load of manure. Camouflaging the milestone under a pile of 'Pigyard Special' for the duration, he maintained that 'They old Nasties would think twice before plastering their jackboots in that'.

The kettle on the hearth wheezed from lack of water and something in the oven began to burn.

I called once more. A man's voice answered. The policeman, purple-faced and with notebook at the ready, came puffing up the path.

To stand arguing with 'the law' seemed futile, with the Grommett's dinner incinerating on the stove. It was while I was rescuing a dried-out rice pudding from the oven that I heard a thudding noise above our heads.

The policeman, investigating, found Mrs Grommett on the floor of the back bedroom, very sick and needing medical help without delay.

She was sure she was dying. Hadn't she seen a magpie perching on the roof that very morn? Before I could get her things together to go to hospital, I was to go downstairs, look in a drawer in the front parlour and find the key to the front door.

I was to make sure that it opened too, because, left to Tom, she would be carted out through the back way like a worn-out hearthrug. When she left her home for the last time she wanted to go out through the front door, dignified and proper, and feet first.

The front parlour had the musty smell of years of unopened Sundays, captured behind the close-curtained windows and the green chenille curtain shrouding the front door.

Disturbing draught-excluding strips of rag and innumerable spiders, I heaved the front door open, just as Tom Grommett came up the garden path.

'Strike me!' he said. 'That door ain't been opened for twenty years.'

Like his mother, he 'couldn't abide the sight nor smell of hospital', so when the ambulance came along I had to promise to stay with her for the journey before she would consent to go.

I stayed in the hospital waiting-room to hear the doctor's diagnosis, and when I was allowed a glimpse of the old lady, I found her more perturbed about 'them young nurses' washing her all over, than the operation she was about to have.

I left as a probationer brought in a tray with ether, soap, hot water and a razor, and as the cubicle curtains closed behind me heard Mrs Grommett complain.

'Darn fine place this is! Can't you tell which

from t'other? I'm a widow woman, not some fella needing a Saturday shave.'

Mrs Grommett made a quick recovery and within a few weeks was back home, prepared to show her scar to her cronies, and several gallstones in a jam jar to anyone who called.

While she had been away, the threatened invasion seemed more likely. Six-foot-high posts were planted in every field and meadow that was large enough for gliders to land in and a new civilian defence force was announced.

Every able-bodied citizen not due for call-up was asked to a gathering in our old village hall, bringing with them such weapons of defence as they could find. Tom Grommett brought his grandfather's old muzzle-loader; there were old rook guns, and to show that he was on our side our parson came prepared to defend Britain with his catapult.

I sat next to Ethel, a girl of my own age, more beautiful than brainy, as we listened to a gentleman in khaki telling us about guerilla warfare, should the enemy strike.

Ethel asked how she was supposed to stop them.

'Delaying tactics,' said the subaltern, leering. 'I suggest "Take one with you" should be your motto.'

Ethel said she didn't want to go.

All unattended vehicles were to be immobilised. This decree led me once more to being a possible entry in the constable's notebook.

Taking cover from a particularly noisy air battle, I had switched off 'Florrie Ford', our extremely ancient tractor, and without removing the rotor arm, dived under the same hedge as the policeman.

I challenged him to start Florrie's engine 'on the handle' if he was able, and he almost burst out of his tunic collar trying, not realising that no Germans would ride on my tractor unless they first discovered the secret of thumping her just above the fuel tap.

I was issued with a tin hat, a stirrup pump and a permit admitting me to any fire, and on nights of 'bomber's moon' that summer, all three were sometimes in use.

Most men in the village did two or three nights Home Guard duty, and knowing that Mrs Grommett was alone on the night that incendiary bombs had set fire to a cornfield close to Chapel End, I slipped across to see if she was safe.

The raid had not upset her, but she was pleased to see me.

'My Lord, girl, 'tis the haunts! I've heard such a scratching and a'screeching, I reckon that Old Nick himself be up the chimney. It keeps smoking something chronic. I've tried putting two pokers crossways in the fire and put handfuls of salt on it to drive the devil away.'

There were peculiar noises coming down the

chimney and I was more than pleased when Tom Grommett, slipping away from his official duties, came in through the back door.

He heard the noises and, 'invasion-minded', wondered if any of 'they old Nasties' had landed and were in the chimney.

'By cripes,' he said. 'I'll give them invasion if they have.'

Grabbing the old muzzle-loader gun, he pointed it up the chimney. The impact of the explosion brought down an avalanche of soot.

'Listen,' said Tom. We, too, could hear something crashing around in the parlour.

'Quick, Tom,' said the old lady. 'If it's Old Nick, or a parachuter, get you through there and chase 'em out through the front door.'

Tom did as he was told, and a bewildered owl flew away.

The sound of gunfire brought Tom's Home Guard companions at the double.

'Have they landed?' someone called through the smoky darkness.

'No,' said Mrs Grommett. 'We've just been caught in a passing shower of soot.'

THE VET'S WEDDING PRESENT

There can be few brides who find it necessary to cycle several miles on their wedding morning, seeking an urgent consultation with the vet.

But I knew that his diagnosis would decide whether the arrangements for the wedding reception could go ahead as planned.

I had been up since before sunrise, hurrying to get the essential chores finished early so that I could concentrate on trying to transform an ugly-duckling farm girl into a swan-like bride.

Of all the mornings of my life, this had to be the one that found Snowdrop, our saddleback sow, staggering around her sty in unsteady circles, very sick indeed.

We had encountered swine fever before, and to see the sow with all the symptoms of the disease brought back memories of quicklime pits, disinfectant troughs, and barred access making for complete isolation of our farm.

The prospect of arriving at the church in bridal gown and disinfected 'wellies' was more than I could bear. Droves of relatives and friends would be arriving for the ceremony later in the day. Thanks to a sick pig there was a distinct possibility that my wedding reception would take place on the grass verge outside the farm gate. It would probably rain.

The cause of the sow's sickness was something that must be immediately identified.

Off I pedalled, anxious to reach the vet before he started his day's rounds and knowing that if he was anywhere within homing distance of the Lockley Arms near opening time he would be immovable as a monolith until 'stop tap' at half-past-two.

At that time, if things went to schedule, I should be going up the aisle.

The old bull-nosed Morris Cowley was outside his house, with both front wheels resting on the porch step. Unshaven, and giving off enough whisky fumes to ignite a spirit lamp, the vet confessed that on the previous night he had forgotten that he was driving and not walking home. The engine had stalled before he could get near enough to unlock the front door.

The canvas hood of the car was down, so dumping my bike in the back and steering a crab-like course along the road, like a sail-boat tacking into the wind, he drove toward the farm.

When we arrived, Snowdrop, the sow, was dead. The vet decided to do an immediate post-mortem.

The wedding reception preparations were in a state of chaos, while I, acting as vet's assistant, trudged around in a cloud of depressing gloom. This deepened as time ticked on with no definite conclusions as to the cause of death.

All brides are supposed to have pre-wedding nerves. I had my touch of the dramatics ankle-deep in gore, with a bass broom and a bucket in my hands.

'I'll soon go as crazy as poor old Snowdrop looked,' I wailed. This suggested a new possibility to the vet. He discovered that the sow's death had been due to some malfunction of the brain.

While I had been helping the vet, Dad had been busy digging a pit, into which Snowdrop was dispatched with almost indecent haste.

It was all signals go for holding the reception at home.

The vet came back into the house to clean up and to collect his fee. This he handed to me as a wedding present.

In those days our local weekly paper printed wedding gift lists. I wondered how 'Vet's gift, professional services—autopsy of a pig' would look in print.

By this time guests were arriving and Mum took Dad off to push, pull, and bully him into his best suit and starched, stiff-fronted white shirt. It was just one frantic rush, but we were only one minute late at the church, and Alan was waiting for me at the altar steps.

When we got back to the reception a helper said that the vet had left two bottles of whisky, with his best wishes for our happiness.

Remembering that when our war-time wedding took place, whisky was as easily available as false teeth for fowls, I still marvel at his generosity, but the vet had always been an enigma to me.

He scarcely inspired professional confidence, for he frequently consulted Bert, the blacksmith, if called on to treat a sick horse.

Some of his methods were antiquated beyond belief. Where one calcium injection could bring almost instantaneous improvement to a cow suffering from mastitis, *his* method was to hold back the flow of milk by inflating the poor thing's udder full of air.

When Dolly, our shorthorn cow, went down with this condition soon after the birth of a heifer calf, the vet treated her in this manner, and gave no hope of saving either cow or calf. He had reckoned without Mum's knowledge of folk medicines, Dad's doggedness and our combined ingenuity.

With no cow's milk and a weakling, wailing

calf to feed, we took a tin of condensed milk, mixed it as per instructions for new-born babies, poured it into a rubber glove and, puncturing the tip of one finger, fed the calf with that.

Mum mixed up a concoction of boiled linseed, black treacle and herbs that looked revolting and smelled worse, but we got it down the cow's throat and worked on, hour after hour, trying to decrease the poor beast's discomfort.

At last she struggled to rise and, prevented from falling and damaging herself by surrounding straw bales, swayed on quivering legs. This was the time to show the calf that there were more interesting milk supplies than rubber gloves.

She drew nothing but air at first, but soon, with a cream moustache around her mouth and replete with her first authentic feed, the calf gave a long and satisfying burp.

The next morning the dog meat cart from the kennels called.

'The vet says that you have a dead cow and calf for us,' the driver said. In unvarnished language, Dad told him where he could take his dog meat cart, with the vet on board as well.

Yet the vet could display infinite patience and kindness with ailing animals and never refused a call for help, unless it came at a time when he had spent too much money and too many hours in the Lockley Arms.

I could not have been more than ten years old when, acting as a messenger for the vet, I first saw Miss Ashstead, an eccentric, who lived at the far end of Plough Lane. Her bungalow was entrenched behind a high, peep-proof fence, topped with a barbed wire trellis.

Callers had to ring a bell on the gate, tradesmen left their deliveries in a cupboard-like box in the gatepost wall, and anyone who tried to venture near the house ran the risk of being savaged by a couple of extremely evil-tempered dogs.

Miss Ashstead never left her fortified home. The only visitors who were admitted were the vet and Ethel Pearce's mother, who washed Miss Ashstead's blankets once a year.

This made Ethel an authority on Miss Ashstead's eccentricity, and through her we heard of foreign, heathen things, like fat old idols, brass gongs, and weirdly carved wooden ornaments.

Tiger-skin rugs, their heads intact with glassy glowing eyes, lurked on the floors and, worse than that, where other people had a parlour table, Miss Ashstead had her coffin, all silk-lined, her name inscribed in the lid, and nonchalantly draped with an Oriental silk shawl.

I felt some alarm when the vet asked me to deliver a bottle of lotion and some medicine to Miss Ashstead's place.

'If she needs a hand, tell her you are used to

animals,' he said, and drove away.

Terrified, I rang the gate bell, delivering the message as I passed the packages through. The bolts were drawn and Miss Ashstead, ogre of my childhood nightmares, turned out to be a timid, tiny woman, devoid of eyebrows or lashes and, I suspect, her own hair.

The sick dog was an ancient, toothless bulldog with eczema. I helped her to dress the dog's sores but, remembering the story of her coffin coffee table, declined the offer of biscuits and lemonade.

I never saw Miss Ashstead again. She died soon after I was married, leaving a considerable sum of money to the vet—who promptly ran off with the barmaid of the Lockley Arms.

It caused a nine-days wonder in the village.

'Drink and that brazen hussy 'ull kill the old vet off,' was the general opinion. But, as Bert said to Dad, 'What a lovely way to go.'

THE CHARCOAL BURNER'S PATH

Generations of village children knew it as 'the charcoal burner's path' and along it, in their various seasons, grew wild strawberries, bilberries, and yellow raspberries.

Each autumn we would scuffle through leaves falling from trees that seemed to reach the sky above our heads, searching, prickly fingered, as we prized the shiny-coated chestnuts from their spiky husks.

To follow the track along the four or five winding woodland miles filled every minute of a summer afternoon. Few of us would admit to having any apprehension about walking along it alone, but by some unspoken understanding we always seemed to go in little groups.

It was not keenness for healthy exercise that

sent us scuttling along the path. We knew that, in addition to the wild fruit that grew along the way, we could gather a free harvest from the overgrown garden of a derelict cottage, miles from anywhere.

In an open clearing, where the timber had most probably been felled to provide material for building, Reeves Cottage stood surrounded by the isolation and silence of tall trees.

Children whose mothers were making jam or jelly were sent there laden with picking baskets and the threat of what would happen to them if they came back with the fruit spilled, squashed or 'finger-blighted' on the way.

Marauding jays and pigeons did their best to strip the trees before we got there, but their success must have been limited, for on the homeward journey of fruit-picking expeditions to Reeves Cottage that I remember, progress was halted through some of the pickers suffering from a surfeit of Amber, or Round-Heart cherries, or enduring stomach ache for believing that the sour Morello cherries tasted 'really lovely' providing that they were reasonably red.

Bindweed, 'Old Man's Beard', and roses that had long since reverted to the briar from which they sprung, provided a living shroud for the crumbling remains of the old wooden cottage. Although the door had long since rotted none of us were brave enough to venture in.

We told each other that, dared-to or not, we could not go inside. Our parents had forbidden it because it wasn't safe. Parental warnings had never bothered any of us overmuch before, but I think each of us recognised that there was an atmosphere so sombre, gloomy, and oppressive, that to venture beyond the threshold gave one instant goose-pimples, even on the hottest summer day.

Reeves Cottage and its surroundings always filled me with an illogical apprehension. If anyone had told me that Goldilocks had her traumatic encounter with the three bears there, I would have believed every word.

Likewise, I was convinced that if war parties of hostile Red Indians no longer roamed the American forests and prairies, it was because they were watching and waiting for me in the eerily silent surrounding wood.

By comparison, my father's explanation of why Reeves Cottage stood where it did seemed very tame indeed.

Built at a time when our woods were still part of a vast royal forest, it had housed the King's Wood Reeve, appointed to prevent commoners stealing the King's wood or his deer. Later on it became a forester's cottage. Dramatically the last tenant had been ambushed on his own doorstep by a gang of poachers, and the place had stood empty for a lifetime.

Followed to its farthest extent, the path led

through the wood to Burner's Meadow. Sometimes here the air would be filled with the pleasant smell of burning turf and oak wood. The charcoal burners would be busy by a fire from which there was never any flame, and seldom more than a wisp of smoke to be seen.

They guarded the secrets of their trade so diligently that anyone, young or old, who ventured near risked being told to go away—in a rather colourful vernacular.

Oak wood cut to uniform lengths was built up around a small but fierce fire. It was then sealed in with layer upon layer of turves that hardened like kilned clay and completely covered in the beehive shaped fire. Until the crust was opened and the charcoaled wood removed, the men would not leave the fire to eat or even sleep.

Many times I have followed the track past Reeves Cottage, both in the reality of childhood and later in my childhood recollections.

'Tell us about the haunted cottage in the wood, Mum,' was a favourite bed-delaying tactic used by my own children. Back I would go along the old familiar path again.

On his last leave, Chris, my son, now tall enough to call his father 'Shorty', confessed to having nightmares about Reeve Cottage when he was small. He wondered if we might go and see if any trace of it still remained.

Once I had become accustomed to the

sensation of bouncing around like a bean in a bucket, riding in Chris's ancient 'banger' was an experience not to be missed.

When we parked, I checked that all my bones were in working order then looked for the old path. The wood was so overgrown that we could not find it, but a firebreak track across the wood-covered hillside seemed to head in the right direction.

We set off, walking on mossy emerald green grass, extremely boggy between ruts cut by heavy forestry tractors, ankle deep in acid, peat-stained water, the colour of cold stewed tea.

We found the old path where the yellow raspberries used to grow and followed it down into a sunless valley that felt as if it had been forest since time began.

The air was heavy with the smell of the fern leaves beneath our feet. Stunted trees that showed no interest in survival were draped in moss and lichens that hung like slumbering bats from the branches around our heads.

In Reeves Cottage clearing, the house had gone back to the earth that bore it, with only the vague outlines of roof rafters to show where it once stood.

Most of the old fruit trees had succumbed to age and tempest, except the gnarled medlar which was still sustained by the hawthorn that had grafted it to life.

Then we found the ancient russet apple tree,

blown down with only half the roots still in the ground. It was laden with tiny green apples.

We sat on its trunk eating our sandwiches. Chris suggested that when his autumn leave came round, we would come back and pick the fruit.

I looked at the withered trees and the dead house. No birds were singing. Goose pimples appeared on my arms. I shivered despite the sun.

'I doubt if we would ever find our way back here,' was the only lame, spur-of-the-moment excuse I could offer. It was time to let the forest take back what belonged to it.

In silence we turned back towards home.

A COMMUNITY MINDED WOMAN

The village football team was never troubled with violence or aggression. Any rival supporters with an inclination to partisan punch-ups, cooled off rapidly as they stood among the boggy rushes round the sidelines, with water seeping through the soles of their muddy shoes.

Players or spectators with aggressive tendencies also knew better than to provoke the wrath of our team's founder, driving force, and manager, Ernie Pearce's Mum.

A highly respected lady of Amazonian proportions, this unlikely patroness of soccer could box an offender's ear with a right jab that flew as fast as a grass snake's flickering tongue. Fighting or fouling players were likely to be

213

hauled off by the scruff of their necks and the back elastic of their shorts, risking a severe thumping before they landed in a wet ditch. Mrs Pearce called it, 'Teaching them to live peaceable.'

The Pearce's lived at Box cottage, a 'two-up, two down and wash-house' little dwelling, with long narrow gardens at both front and rear.

Where other villagers grew Bramley apples and Conference pears, the trees at Mrs Pearce's sprouted a multitude of clothes lines. Supported by wooden clothes props, each bore a crop of dolly pegs.

Around the time that the team was first founded, life for Ernie and his younger sister, Ethel, was dominated by the need to pump up water, stoke the copper fire, and stir the lumps out of endless and enormous bowls of starch.

With Ernie's wages as a gardener's lad a mere pittance, and no husband to support them, Mrs Pearce fought off poverty by washing for an extensive clientele.

Her skill as a laundress was so well recognised that a spell of damp, drizzling, rainy weather would be commented on locally as being 'shocking bad for Mrs Pearce'.

Many lady visitors tried to discover the secret of how she could transform crumpled laundry into immaculately white linen, but any attempt to get beyond the glass-beaded curtain screening off the front parlour found Mrs Pearce's bulky figure blocking their vision beyond the wash-house door.

Because I was just the kid from the farm, delivering skimmed milk in an enamel can every morning, I was permitted in the wash-house and, as a special favour, was allowed to help Ethel deliver the washing on her way to school.

Perhaps her mother knew I was too scared of her to divulge that she made blankets soft and fluffy by adding ammonia to the water they were washed in, plus a spoonful of olive oil in their final rinse.

The ladies who wondered how she achieved such pristine whiteness on her wash lines knew nothing of the buckets of rainwater soaking and infiltrating through a barrel of wood ash and coming through the bored holes in the bottom as lye. Strained through muslin, the resultant liquid was used to steep table damasks, napery, and sheets.

There was always an elusive scent of wild violets and wet fern leaves that clung to everything the washerwoman laundered, yet her customers never knew that orris root in the rinsing water gave it a country fragrance of its own.

In the bricked-in copper that filled one corner of the wash-house, the washing plopped and walloped like an erupting geyser as it boiled, spreading mists of steam.

Beads of condensation clung to the asthmatically-creaking water-pump above the deep earthenware sink. With each iron cog protesting at the load that was being forced through its wooden rollers, the handle of the heavy old iron-framed mangle by the door submitted to the strength of Mrs Pearce's arms.

Summer and winter the kitchen was a stuffy inferno. On racks suspended from the low ceiling, airing washing successfully hampered the invasion of fresh air. Angels would not have dared brush their wings against it as it swung at less than shoulder height.

Flat-irons of every size and weight stood on the hob plate, with their noses pressed against the red-glowing fire bars. 'Goffering' tongs, used to crimp lace and the frills on maids caps and aprons, lay heating on the top of the stove. A wax candle was kept handy to impart a gloss on stiff collars and shirt fronts.

When 'six of everything and a dozen of most' was the target aimed for in any self-respecting girl's trousseau, garments made to wear well, in good 'no-nonsense' materials, often outlasted their owners. For this reason Mrs Pearce had 'inherited' a large bundle of clothes.

It contained twelve voluminous pairs of cotton twill bloomers, with crochet-edge frilling around each leg. Ernie, whose one relaxation was to play football with the lads of the village, with coats as goalposts, remarked that, pruned back, they would supply a football team with shorts.

Of such chance remarks are inspirations founded. Mrs Pearce, shrewdly realising that muddy pitches make plenty of washing, prevailed on her customers to contribute towards buying a football and even approached 'The Hall' for funds and support. 'A community-minded woman', His Lordship called her, topping the fund with half-a-sovereign and instructing the estate carpenter to get a pair of goalposts made. Goat nets were a luxury that could be dispensed with. Since most lads wore sturdy hobnailed boots and thick, knitted socks anyway, all that was needed was eleven jerseys and the volunteers to fill them, and the village would have a football team.

Ernie's uncle, working for a coastal urban council, found that their bathing costume service was being discontinued and snapped up a job lot of 'unused Gents' bathing suits. They were striped in bands of black and yellow with elbow-length sleeves.

Ethel, handy with a needle, chopped off the legs and finished off the jerseys with a narrow hem. Using her brother as a pattern, she hacked the frills from the legs of the bloomers and made all twelve pairs to hang loose and floppy just above his knees.

Those who wanted to join the team assembled at Box Cottage for the issue and trying on of kit.

Ernie, a well-built lad and tall for his sixteen

summers, was first one out of his wash-house changing room. His jersey and shorts were more than generously proportioned. Shorter, skinnier lads emerged with the legs of their shorts covering their kneecaps and the wasp-striped jerseys hanging like knee-length frocks.

Mrs Pearce informed them that they looked a real treat and that any slight fullness in the material would take up in the wash.

Every Monday morning in winter the lines in Box Cottage garden would flap with shorts and ever-lengthening shirts.

When war sent Ernie and most of the team into the forces, the goalposts were put in the tythe barn for safe keeping. The football kits were washed, ironed and packed away waiting for peace. But our team, like Ernie, was one of the casualties of the war.

An attempt was made to revive it, but the physical training instructor who tried was not in Ernie's Mum's league when it came to winning matches and encouraging the team.

So enthusiasm dwindled and expired, ducks and geese could go for Saturday afternoon swims on the centre line undisturbed.

Even now, it takes but little imagination as you pass the modernised, landscaped garden of Box Cottage to see a line of droopy cotton twill shorts and sagging stockingette jerseys, sighing and flapping in the breeze.

THE OTHER HALF

I am not certain when it was that Charlie Cartwright entered two Aberdeen Angus steers in the Smithfield Show. I do know that some of the more adventurous among us made it an excuse to go to London to give token support, and to see for ourselves how the other, more sophisticated, half of the population lived.

Unconvinced that the mainline express we had boarded at the junction was really London-bound and not hurtling us towards some outlandish destination, we tried to read the place names of gas-lit stations as the train steamed through.

It took two reassuring ticket collectors, and a near decapitation, before everyone relaxed enough to look through steamy windows in the first dim light of day and discuss 'up country' farm land that we considered inferior to our own.

Approaching the grimy heart of London, we marvelled that the inhabitants ever found enough fresh air to breathe.

One of our number actually understood the intricacies of the London Underground railway. Like a flock of frightened sheep in a strange pasture, we followed our shepherding pathfinder mighty close.

Caught up in the crush and bustle of a rush-hour tube train, Wally Skinner, in doom-laden tones of amazing audibility, informed a carriage full of city workers that: 'Only unnatural folk would go burrowing around through miles of underground tunnels like a lot of scuttly, little old moles.'

Smithfield at last, where some members of the excursion were content to spend the whole of the day.

Others, with implicit faith in providence and the Metropolitan Police went off sight seeing; while a really adventurous contingent went Christmas window-shopping in the West End stores.

The displays were overwhelming. So were some of the prices. One hauled-along husband, goggle-eyed at the price of a flimsy garment, informed a group of elegantly-groomed salesladies hovering near him that he had paid less than that for two top-grade in-calf cows.

Haughty glances swept scornfully towards our little group and at that moment I was sure all London knew my outfit started out as an end-of-roll bargain remnant, allied to a free pattern from a two-year-old magazine.

Reassembled, our little company mustered in the foyer of a theatre and trooped up endless flights of stairs. High in the gallery, perched like thatchers working on a steep-pitched roof, we were caught up in a tide of music, colour, and artistry that still flooded over us when we were back outside in the cold night air.

Content to dream and doze, we watched the glow of the lamplit city slip past the train windows and turn to the star-bright dark of a country sky.

Long past midnight, with my footsteps echoing through the shadowed quietness, I realised that in comparison with the Christmas-decorated streets of the city, the tarnished tinsel that was the full extent of the festive display in the village shop-cum-post office, would look very subdued indeed.

Similarly, with the music and gaiety of the theatre production still indelibly in our minds, those who went to the rehearsal of our annual Christmas concert on the following evening faced the reality that our forthcoming production had the zest and sparkle of an old and tough dead duck.

It needed light and colour, and something better in the way of music. What we had was a damp-warped piano with two notes missing, overhead oil lamps for illumination, and acoustic-muffling curtains like rejected Army blankets dipped in elderberry dye. They were blotched with mildew and, pulled back to hide their defects, had the disconcerting knack of falling down.

The Maiden's Prayer, *Clementine*, and *Poor Old Joe* were not the songs to set feet tapping. A sketch wherein the part of the wicked, land-owning squire had to be rewritten so as not to give offence to His Lordship, was hardly likely to rivet an audience spellbound to their seats.

The rehearsal became a discussion on how to alter the planned routine. The parson and the preacher from the chapel were both present, the former appalled that we had been affected by Babylonian places of pleasure, the latter agreeing that some cheerful choruses and even dancing would not be amiss, providing that no young females pranced around flaunting their stocking-tops.

It was decided that the school-children's Nativity play that usually took place during school hours, would be performed as the first half of the concert. They alone would help provide some of the spontaneity it lacked.

The volume, if not the quality of the music, could be improved if we could get Dick, the roadman, to bring his fiddle. Old Dubber Wall would play his melodion, bribed with the promise of a pint. The gatekeeper over at

Tylers Halt crossing was always eager to play his bagpipes, and Wally Skinner would improvise on his harmonica to help the good cause. He knew of a fellow farmhand with a good deep baritone voice, but because he was a refugee from war-torn Europe, his knowledge of our language was sparse.

On the concert night the hall was packed. Anyone with the slightest glimmer of talent had been urged to join in. On a stage lit by headlamps linked to a couple of car batteries, a small Joseph nudged a minute Mary. Cuddling a swaddling-wrapped dolly close to her, she looked at her Mum in the front row of the audience and, gaining reassurance from watching her mother's mouth moving in unison, went breathlessly through her lines.

White-nightied angels jostled Herod's cardboard-armoured soldiers to get to the front of the stage and wave to familiar faces beyond the lights. Yet the simplicity of their treble voices brought out the point that long ago in a far-off country, a child was born among folk who, like us, tended flocks.

The second half of the programme was made up of sketches, a whistle through 'A Monastery Garden', step dancing to Dubber Wall's melodion, and a bit of choral singing to pad it out. The crossing keeper's bagpipes had a touch of croup about them, and no one really minded when he had to cut his recital short to slip away and let the 'Ten-nineteen' through.

223

Dick, the roadman, carrying his fiddle, introduced the refugee singer to the audience as Tommy Slav, since no one could pronounce his proper name. At first Dick tried to tune his fiddle to the notes of the piano. But Tommy Slav took it gently from him, tightened the strings and began to play.

Our village hall was crammed with everyday country people, unversed in the knowledge of music, yet we knew that we were listening to an artist who could make Dick's old fiddle weep for a people subjugated and far away.

We sat in silence and he played on long after the flattened batteries made the stage lights dim.

Our old hut was filled with magic and melody. At last, bowing and handing Dick back his fiddle, Tommy Slav left the stage, went out of the side door and was gone. Only then did the hall erupt in spontaneous appreciation, and Dick, staring at his old fiddle, said quietly:

'I don't reckon any of us knows just how the other half lives.'

OLD HARRY

Ask old Harry Applethorn to tell you about his boyhood and early working life and he will say that they were one and the same thing.

Behind the phrase that he had 'no parents to speak of', lies the heartbreak of a neglected, unloved child, 'raised up' by three old bachelor uncles and a spinster aunt.

Their home was a clay-floored, stone-walled hovel at the end of a lonely farm track where the bare-foot child wandered in and out as freely as the chickens, backyard piglets, and half wild cats.

He picked himself up when he fell over, slept on a straw palliasse on a shelf of the chimney corner cupboard, and seldom encountered any other company but that of his uncles and aunt.

Authority descended on the cottage when a school attendance officer arrived, demanding to know the reason why Harry was not attending school.

Compulsory education had been introduced after Harry's relatives had passed the 'age of fighting and making pothooks'; they had no idea that they were breaking the law by not sending him to school.

Until then, like all small children of humble country labourers, Harry had been trotting around 'un-breeched' Although boys and girls alike were muffled in layers of petticoats, they were kept bare-bottomed until they learned the comfort of keeping 'dry' and clean.

Harry's aunt overcame the problem of 'breeching' him to start school the next morning, by simply sewing him into a pair of his uncle's flap-fronted fustian trousers, with the legs cut short.

Sheepswool stuffed into a pair of his aunt's button-up boots helped prevent his feet from walking out of them. With his pinafore and petticoats tucked into his low-crotched breeches, Harry was sent off alone to walk the three cross-country miles to school.

He had never ventured so far afield before. Getting lost made him commit the unpardonable sin of being late for school on his first day.

Reaching tip-toe to the latch of the schoolroom door, Harry pushed it open, hesitantly entering a strange terrifying hell.

Bawled at by a bullying sadistic schoolmaster, jeered at by more children than he had ever imagined to exist, Harry spent that first miserable morning standing on a stool in the corner of the classroom.

Trudging home in the winter twilight along gloomy woodland paths, past rustling hedgerows of the mist enshrouded meadows, Harry was stalked by nameless, goblin-haunted terrors that hovered just behind him, waiting to grab him as he ran.

Knowing that his aunt kept ghosts and witches away from the cottage by placing saucers of salt on the hearth and threshold each All Soul's Eve, Harry carried a small lump of salt which he had taken from the brine barrel when his uncles were pig killing that autumn. He hoped it might give him some measure of protection, but it only dissolved in his ever damp clothing and Harry scuttled along with his constant cold weather companion, fear.

Life was much happier in spring and summer. His uncles and other farm men working in the fields would watch out for him going to school and call him to lead the horse 'shimming' turnips, or ride on the back bar of the corn drill to ensure that the seeds were falling down through the funnels and spouts without their becoming blocked.

When the reapers were in the cornfields he would be hailed to go bond making and tying sheaves or lead the huge Shirehorses that pulled the harvest wagons. It seemed worth all the beatings, canings, and screamed abuse that the schoolmaster awarded him for his truancy, when grown men praised his skill at handling a horse.

Harry was rising twelve when Queen Victoria's Diamond Jubilee was celebrated. For weeks the dull routine of school had been enlivened by rehearsals of tableaux, patriotic songs, and recitations, to be performed at a village gala on the morning of the great day.

Strictly sectarian and narrow, his aunt said she would as soon sew him a winding sheet as she would lift a needle to make a fancy costume for him to go 'play acting' in public at the village hall. Opting out of trying to be 'Jolly Jack Tar' and attempting a sailors horn pipe in his handed-down trousers and 'clout nailed' boots, Harry skipped the Jubilee Day performance. Instead, he accepted the Manor groom's invitation to help him poultice a lame mare.

Everyone attended the afternoon Jubilee tea party. Each pupil on the school register was mustered to receive a medal and a mug. Harry lined up with them, looking at the laden trestle tables all around him. An unrecognisable substance, glistening and quivering in great glass dishes, looked rather like the gum from plum trees, except that it was green, yellow, and red.

Someone told him it was 'jelly' and that they were going to eat it. Harry's mouth watered at the thought.

There were also iced cakes, white as if they had just been snowed on. Harry wondered how whoever had made them, managed to find frost and ice in warm weather, and why the ice cakes had not melted on the plates. His anticipation of new gastronomic experiences made his stomach rumble as the line moved slowly on.

The girls in front of Harry were congratulated on their school and church attendance. Then, having been presented with mugs and medals, they moved to the table and sat down.

Harry stepped forward, bowing clumsily, with his hand extended. He was offered nothing. Instead, the schoolmaster announced that he would be failing in both his patriotic and his Christian duties, not to make an example and draw public attention to this miserable youth.

Harry's failure to take part in the school's loyal tribute, plus his persistent truancy, now disbarred him from having any part in the day's events. No medal, no mug, no tea!

Scarlet with humiliation, Harry ran, and kept on running. His Jubilee tea was a raw turnip eaten in the straw-warmed darkness of an isolated barn.

By the following evening, Harry was approaching the first big town he had ever seen. Ahead lay gas-lit streets, loud music, and people shouting. Turning a corner, Harry got his first glimpse of a travelling fair.

The menagerie and side shows offered wonders Harry had never dreamed of. The sound of the mighty steam organ held him enthralled. Approaching a man who seemed to be the 'gaffer', Harry asked if there was any work going for a strong and able fifteen-year-old boy.

He was set to work on the sideshows. When enough people had paid their money to see the spectacle of 'The Man Eating Cow', Harry's task was to sit on the tiny stage munching a cow heel. He became adept at dodging the missiles that the angry patrons threw.

During this performance, the barkers and drummers in front of the adjoining tent were urging customers to view 'The Great Pan, Half A Goat And Half A Man'.

Ducking through the canvas tent walls to stand behind a waist-high screen, clutching an enormous frying pan, Harry shared the stage with a goat tethered so that only its rear end was on show!

Fights with knives and fists were frequent and life was rough. But the anonymity of the travelling fair suited Harry and he stayed with it for a couple of years.

En route from one town to the next, he sat down to rest at the kerbside of a residential street when a hard-driven cob and trap drew up beside him.

A gentleman in a swallow-tailed coat and top hat offered him sixpence to mind the horse for a quarter of an hour. It seemed an easy way to earn a 'tanner', but fifteen minutes drifted into a wet half-hour, extending into an hour.

Apologizing profusely, the gentleman offered him a florin, but received in return a lecture on the sheer stupidity of leaving a sweating horse to stand shivering in the rain.

'You're right, boy! But I'm a doctor and I couldn't tell the baby I was delivering to wait a while until I'd stabled the horse—well could I! If you are looking for honest work, I'm looking for an honest groom.'

So Harry found a new job and a new way of life. Never before had he experienced good food, warm lodgings, and the undreamed-of luxury of sleeping between clean white sheets in a comfortable bed.

Happy as a porker in an oak forest, Harry drove the old doctor on his rounds. Regardless of their ailments, his patients always expected to be given a bottle of medicine. These Harry helped to dispense. The recipe was always the same. One gallon of water added to eight ounces of Epsom Salts was coloured with 'Black Jack'—burnt brown sugar—for private paying patients. Those on the doctor's 'halfpenny club', had to take it plain.

When the doctor found Harry pounding brimstone and wild garlic together to make parasite repellant pellets for the horse he hailed the prescription as Nature's cure for all humanity's ailments. The sick in the district were instructed to take them 'One after meals, three times a day'.

Their effect bordered on the miraculous. Even those with long-standing ailments pronounced themselves cured, having no need to bother the doctor again.

The memory of the old doctor's cure-all pills still makes Harry's mouth go dry. Three quarters of a century later his lined old face wrinkles with recollection, like a dry, anaemic prune.

'Of course, by that time,' Harry recalled, 'Them old Boers were being a bit of a nuisance, so I joined the army, but I only stayed a soldier for one week. The recruiting sergeant who had persuaded me to take the Queen's shilling, found out my proper age, just fifteen years old and took the shilling back. All I got for being patriotic was a hiding. They told me to remuster when the cradle marks were off my bum, but I didn't! I saw enough of the army to know that soldiering was no life for me.'

Harry returned to the old doctor, but the practice had almost dwindled into non-existence, since he was often too tipsy to sit upright in the cart. Harry knew that he must start looking for another job.

In actual fact, the job found him. Taking the cob to the farrier one morning, he met the smith's apprentice running panic-stricken along the village street.

'Don't 'ee bring yon mare down to the smithy, Harry! We've got a tarnation grut Clydesdale in there, roaring mad, and kicking the place to Kingdom Come!'

Tying the cob to the hitching ring on the inn yard wall, Harry ran to the smithy to find the smith retching and winded, having been hurled through the door.

Shaking as if stricken by the palsy, and mopping up the blood that poured from a hoof-gashed cheek, the elderly man in charge of the stallion stood beside him, complaining that he had warned his master that the 'entire' was getting too full of himself to handle, but that no one else had been set on to take his place.

To the accompaniment of crashing hooves and splintering woodwork, the blacksmith acknowledged that Harry had 'a way with horses', and offered him half a sovereign if he could either get a choke rope round the brute's neck, or quieten it down.

Harry had not worked among the old farm horsemen and the fairground travellers without picking up a few tips about horse 'doctoring'. He knew the gipsy methods for quieting horses, or making them go, and to this end always carried two tiny bottles of 'something special' in his 'weskit' pocket.

Smearing some drops of liquid from one of

233

his bottles on to his hands and on the lining of his hard hat, he tossed the hat through the open shutter to land close by the stallion's plunging head. The flattened ears twitched, the flared nostrils quivered, the arched neck turned in enquiry. Clambering in through the shutters, talking quietly, Harry approached the stallion with outstretched hands, showing no fear.

Stroking neck and sweat-flecked withers, Harry calmed the rampaging stallion until it stood placidly while he put on its halter and bit.

It took all his powers of persuasion to make the smith believe that the horse would stand quietly to be shod, but it did.

Perhaps that was the start of Harry being known as a 'horse whisperer'. I knew that he had that reputation when I was young, so I asked him what he had kept in his waistcoat pocket all those years ago.

'Things "greeable" to horses!' was the non-committal answer.

When I asked him to be more specific, he informed me that I was always 'a-worriting' and wanting to know the 'whys and wherefores' when I was a pestering young 'un, and there were some folks that didn't improve with age!

He did admit that 'They old horses were something partial to sweetcake, oil of cinnamon, fennel, and a few other things he could mention'.

He had dosed more than a few dozy nags

with 'red dragon', black powder, flowers of brimstone, and boiled linseed in his time.

By the time the smithy had been restored to some semblance of order, the stallion's owner had arrived.

Its 'leader', still shaken, admitted that he had been in mortal fear of the 'entire' for some time, and now the creature knew it. All he wanted to do was to quit and find a quieter job.

The smith suggested that the solution to all their problems was that Harry and the stallion's leader should change jobs.

Under Harry's care, the stallion became a magnificent creature, winning awards and cups by the dozen. Harry travelled from farm to farm with the stallion. This was his life until he married, at twenty-five, and decided it was time to settle down.

His next job was on an arable farm of some four hundred acres, eventually becoming leading horseman.

It was a calling Harry was proud of, but the year was 1915, and the furnaces of war needed to be stoked both with horses and with men.

Watching his best teams being requisitioned, Harry, at thirty, joined the Veterinary Corps.

The plight of the horses floundering through the battle fields of Europe appalled him. It seemed wanton wickedness to watch fine bloodstock, and worn out, broken-kneed old nags, driven relentlessly until they dropped dead, or were shot where they lay, too exhausted to struggle on in the Flanders mud.

Harry was hit by a sniper's bullet as he tried to rescue a drowning mare from a shell crater. He was invalided home.

His old job had gone, and for a few years Harry had to take work as and when he could find it. Then, in the year that I was born, Harry and his gentle wife moved into the cottage by our farm.

As my father's wagoner, his pay was less than magnificent but there was always an amiable atmosphere about the place. The only cloud on the horizon of the couple's happiness was that they were childless. It was an emptiness that went unappeased until one bleak wintry day when a bedraggled boy came limping into our lives.

If Harry saw a reflected echo of his own boyhood, his wife's mind may have dwelt on the son she could never have. On that day when Jamie came hobbling across a muddy field and into the Applethorn's hearts I was privileged to be there.

Not that I thought it much of a privilege at the time. Helping to sort, grade and bag potatoes from a field clamp on a bleak wintry day was not my idea of a cheerful pastime, but my parents firmly believed that Satan would always find work for idle hands. Since they had no intention of supplying hell with labourers I was out there with Dad, Harry Applethorn, and his wife.

Little hands could pick up small potatoes, so with a sack 'apron' round my middle, my feet numb in mud-caked boots, and my black-edged finger nails mourning the loss of circulation in my soil-grimed hands, I sat on an upturned basket, putting under-sized King Edwards into sacks.

It was a well-known country belief that anyone could 'eat a peck of dirt' before they died, so disregarding the grubby state of our hands, except for a token wipe on our soil-clogged aprons, we stood in anticipation of warm food and drink when we saw Mum coming through the gate carrying the pasty basket and the old blue jug.

But Mum seemed to be in no hurry to hand out cheese pasties or hot cocoa.

Instead she stood telling Harry's wife about a half-starved looking lad she had just passed in the lane. As she spoke, the boy came limping across the rough ground towards us. Hatless, his dark hair hung like old thatch round his ears and his enormous dark brown eyes accentuated the thin pallor of his face. His wrists and ankles extended way beyond the thin flannel suit he was wearing. He had over-large and disintegrating boots on his feet.

He asked if we knew if the boss was taking on extra labour to clear the potato clamp. With rain on the wind Dad thought that every potato bagged would be one less to get wet so offered him a day's work at the recognised 'under eighteen' casual labour rate.

'I'll do a man's work and earn a man's pay, mister, because I need the money.' So saying Jamie pitched in to work.

Mum picked up the pasty basket again, saying:

'Now that's settled, I'll share the food round. Would you like a drink of hot cocoa, son?'

Mum's thick, full-bodied cocoa was no drink for the squeamish, often having great globules of fat floating on the surface. Out of her hearing we referred to it as 'Drink-and-be-thankful'. Harry Applethorn reckoned it would 'put a lining on the innards of an ox'. Yet this Jamie was savouring every mouthful as if it was something wonderful. Mum gave him a second cup.

Dad maintained that stooping always played havoc with his appetite, and I noticed Mum break my hot cheese pasty in half. Harry and his wife both professed to have gone off their feed too. Three and a half pasties were left lying in their tea towel wrapper.

'Bother!' said Mum. 'Now I shall have to take them home!'

My offer to help out by eating my full share and someone else's was cut short by Mum's elbow prodding my ribs. I could see no reason for this sort of treatment, and if I begrudged Jamie eating all our 'elevenses' it was simply because I had never come face-to-face with utter starvation before.

As Jamie ate, Mum made him a potato-sack apron and a corn-sack hood to keep the wind off. As she put it round him she realised that his clothing was soaking wet.

Having found a job, Jamie was determined that wet clothes were not going to stop him from earning money.

Poverty was no stranger to farm hands in the early nineteen thirties, but this pathetic young tramp so wrenched at Mum's and Mrs Applethorn's heartstrings that they worked beside him, trying to shelter him from the wind. With their gentle kindness melting Jamie's reserved nature we listened as he told how he came to be walking the roads.

Jamie had an unemployed father who habitually drowned his sense of failure, and his dole money, in a tankard. When Jamie came home from school on his fourteenth birthday, his father told him he would no longer keep him. With several smaller brothers and sisters to be fed, it was time that Jamie left home and got a job.

Three unsuccessful days and sixty miles later, his search for work brought him to our potato field, without any solid food inside him since he had finished the half loaf his cowed mother had smuggled out to him as he left home.

Laying amongst the straw and soil around the potato clamp was a piece of broken harness leather. Jamie picked it up. Dad and Harry both noticed, but said nothing. They were too intent on trying to beat the bad weather, sustained by another 'cocoa and pasties' break from Mum.

It was Mum who first noticed blood on the straw. She nudged Harry.

'Let's take a look at those feet of yours, old son!' he said, brooking no argument. Jamie had walked through his cardboard-lined boots and the soles of his feet as well. It would take more than a piece of perished leather to mend them.

Mum and Mrs Applethorn, both near to tears, bound his feet with strips of cloth torn from the pasty wrapper. A steady chilling drizzle was falling, putting an end to potato sorting for that day.

As Jamie rode home in the wagon with Mum, Mrs Applethorn and me, Dad and Harry, walking beside the horse, considered what to do next. Harry said that if Dad could find some light work for the lad, he and his wife would find him food and shelter.

'My missus is always maundering on about having neither chick nor child to make a fuss of, and personally I reckon that lad needs all the fussing she can spare.'

So Jamie stayed on, becoming the Applethorn's unofficially adopted son. He was held in great affection by my parents, and doted on by both Harry and his wife as he grew to manhood.

Later on, it became increasingly difficult to find the money to pay the wages of Harry and Jamie. So Harry got a job driving a brewery four-horse dray and Jamie joined the Army. The Applethorns still lived in the cottage, and gave us news of Jamie from the letters that they received each week.

When the war broke out, Jamie was among the first to go to France. He was captured in 1940, making the transcontinental journey to Poland as a P.O.W. in an open cattle truck. The fact that a card from him said that he was doing 'land work' offered some consolation to the Applethorns.

People who tilled the land were usually peaceable folk so maybe, we thought, captivity would not lay too heavy a yoke on Jamie's back. Then another letter told them the true state of affairs.

'I often dream of being fourteen and clamping potatoes without a basket or jug,' it said.

We realised then that Jamie was hungry again.

Two years of silence followed. Always as quiet and unassuming as a hen robin Harry's wife became more silent and withdrawn, shutting herself in to polish and clean the spotless second bedroom, waiting for James to come home.

In the face of the Russian advance westward,

the Allied P.O.W.s were withdrawn from Poland and East Germany and herded together to undertake the notorious forced march across Europe. To drop out was to perish, so Jamie kept doggedly walking until the column met up with the Americans. At that moment of liberation Jamie, suffering from pneumonia and tuberculosis, collapsed and died.

Within a month of losing his 'adopted son', Harry lost his wife as well. Only those who knew him well, and possibly the four magnificent Percheron horses he was in charge of, ever saw the depth of Harry's grief.

He was nearer seventy than sixty when a competitor took over the town brewery and promptly closed it.

After that Harry officially retired from work. Not that it stopped him being busy whenever a horse owner in the locality wanted expert help to get a hunter or show jumper ready for show.

I admit to weeping unashamedly as Harry, approaching ninety years of age, and proudly wearing the horseman's rig he purchased in the Edwardian era, led a champion prize winner round the ring.

To me he has always seemed rock-like, wise, as indestructible as Time. He shrugs off the years like passing showers, his mind still blessed with a clarity that makes it a treasure house, storing the remembrance and knowledge of the old ways. He has sublime faith in his future, asking only that when he sets off on his final journey to eternity, he goes garbed in the horseman's outfit which has for so many years been safely stored in the wooden box by his bed.

There will be no cars in Harry's heaven, and he is convinced that horses graze the pastures of paradise.